Zizek and the Rhetorical Unconscious

Robert Samuels

Zizek and the Rhetorical Unconscious

Global Politics, Philosophy, and Subjectivity

palgrave
macmillan

Robert Samuels
Writing Program
University of California, Santa Barbara
Goleta, CA, USA

ISBN 978-3-030-50909-5 ISBN 978-3-030-50910-1 (eBook)
https://doi.org/10.1007/978-3-030-50910-1

This Palgrave Macmillan imprint is published by the registered company Springer Nature Switzerland AG.
The registered company address is: Gewerbestrasse 11, 6330 Cham, Switzerland

Contents

CHAPTER 1

Introduction

Abstract The book uses a critique of Slavoj Zizek's work in order to outline a theory of psychoanalytic rhetoric. I turn to Zizek because not only is he one of the most popular intellectuals in the world, but his discourse is shaped by a set of unconscious rhetorical processes that also determine much of contemporary of politics, culture, and subjectivity. Just as Aristotle argued that the three main forms of persuasion are logos (reason), pathos (emotion), and ethos (authority), I posit that each one of these aspects of communication is related to a fundamental psychoanalytic concept. Moreover, I turn to Aristotle's work on theater to posit a fourth form of rhetoric, catharsis, which is the purging of feelings of fear and pity.

Keywords Zizek • Rhetoric • Ethos • Pathos • Catharsis • Logos

This book uses a critique of Slavoj Zizek's work in order to outline a theory of psychoanalytic rhetoric. I turn to Zizek because not only is he one of the most popular intellectuals in the world, but his discourse is shaped by a set of unconscious rhetorical processes that also determine much of contemporary of politics, culture, and subjectivity.[1] Just as Aristotle argued that the three main forms of persuasion are logos (reason), pathos (emotion), and ethos (authority), I posit that each one of these aspects of communication is related to a fundamental psychoanalytic concept.[2] Moreover,

R. Samuels, *Zizek and the Rhetorical Unconscious*,
https://doi.org/10.1007/978-3-030-50910-1_1

I turn to Aristotle's work on theater to posit a fourth form of rhetoric, catharsis, which is the purging of feelings of fear and pity.[3]

Freud called his initial psychoanalytic method, catharsis, and he argued that the fundamental drive of all human beings is the pleasure principle as the desire to avoid all tension and excessive stimulation.[4] As a form of unconscious rhetoric, catharsis represents a desire to attain pleasure by escaping feelings of guilt and shame. Thus, according to the dictates of the pleasure principle, language can be utilized as a medium for reducing the need for mental energy, and popular culture is fundamentally shaped by the desire to escape from anxiety caused by conflict. Just as people turn to their iPhones or opiates in order to stop thinking about the reality of their lives, catharsis through entertainment allows people the possibility to deny feelings of anxiety, guilt, and shame as they receive instant access to pleasure.

In Zizek's work, we will see how his use of jokes, popular culture, and obscenities helps him to deliver pleasure to his audience, and as Freud argued in relation to jokes, the speaker bribes the audience with enjoyment so that he or she will not be held accountable for what is being said.[5] Jokes, then, provide a safe social space where people are able to express their violent and sexual impulses in a sublimated fashion without fear of retribution. In the context of contemporary culture, we find that entertainment reduces the tension caused by the central conflict between nature and culture. Since society is structured around the regulation of sex and violence, humans have to sacrifice part of their own inner nature to be members of a culture, but as Freud insisted, these natural urges can never be fully effaced, and so they have to be displaced through the use of symbolic substitutions.[6]

It is my contention that we need this theory of catharsis to explain how someone like Donald Trump became president of the United States. From this perspective, we cannot understand his popularity simply by seeing how he caters to certain groups (Christian fundamentalists, nationalists, libertarians, wealthy business people, and the white working class); moreover, the Right's opposition to the Left, to liberals, and the Democrats only represents one aspect of contemporary political polarization.[7] What we get from the theory of catharsis is the extra thing that fuels the Right's hegemonic coalition.

In his first important book, *The Sublime Object of Ideology*, Zizek calls this special connecting force, enjoyment, but I would like to use Freud's original theory of the pleasure principle to replace enjoyment with catharsis.[8] While enjoyment is associated with positive feelings, pleasure has to do with the escape from guilt, shame, and ultimately reality.

We shall see that what Trump embodies is the contemporary blending of capitalism, art, and politics, which were once thought to be separate and opposed areas of culture and everyday life.[9] It is therefore impossible to tell if Trump is a politician or a media star or a businessman because he is all of these things at once, and since entertainment is driven by the delivery of catharsis to its audience, a society where entertainment has spread to most aspects of life is a society shaped by the pleasure principle.

As I show in Chap. 2, it is vital to understand how catharsis works because so much of our culture, politics, and subjectivity is shaped by this unconscious use of rhetoric. As politics becomes a form of entertainment, and the news becomes another mode of art, we see that catharsis enters different aspects of our lives. Moreover, whether we look at the opiate epidemic, the rise of Trump, and or the hypnotic effect of iPhones, we find the same desire of people to escape from reality by accessing an easy and immediate form of pleasure.[10] In examining Zizek's rhetoric, I will demonstrate the role played by catharsis in contemporary culture.

After I elaborate the psychoanalytic rhetorical theory of catharsis, I turn to the use of pathos in contemporary politics, culture, and subjectivity. Drawing from Freud's conception of hysteria, I center my attention on the generation of emotions through the formation of unconscious fantasies. One of my central claims is that you cannot understand politics today if you do not see how pathos is produced through the unconscious mechanisms of victim identity and identification.[11] I not only examine Zizek's use of pathos to gain the attention of his audience, but also argue that necessary minority-based social movements often rely on pathos to create group solidarity. One of the results of this reliance on unconscious emotion is that these collective organizations can become divisive, irrational, and extreme. However, my goal is not to dismiss the need for these movements; rather, I use a psychoanalytic understanding of pathos to elaborate how they can at times become counter-productive.

The use of catharsis and pathos is combined in Chap. 4 with a focus on ethos. Many people believe that ethos represents ethics, but if we read Aristotle's *Rhetoric*, we find that it is clearly based on the role of the speaker as an authority in a particular social context.[12] From the perspective of psychoanalysis and contemporary culture, we have to understand authority and authorship through the concepts of transference and narcissism. Furthermore, in a post-patriarchal culture, we shall see that society is centered on a cynical conformity to dead premodern traditions and beliefs.[13] In Zizek's case, his turn to Hegel exposes the ideological foundations of philosophy and liberal cynicism.

I argue throughout this book that much of Zizek's discourse represents a conflicted relation to psychoanalysis, and in Chap. 5, I elaborate Freud's conception of logos as represented by his theory of the reality principle.[14] For Freud, the neutrality of the analyst and the free association of the patient open up the possibility for a science of everyday life where reason, reality-testing, and impartiality are employed to confront the reality of internal and external conflicts.[15] Thus in opposition to the Imaginary overcoming of difference and conflict, psychoanalysis represents a discourse of radical self-honesty, and this discourse provides a key to understanding the role of modern science and democracy in our globalizing world.

Zizek's rhetoric often goes against modern logos because he argues that it is impossible to approach reality with a neutral, objective perspective. In fact, for Zizek, the Real itself is divided and lacking, and so we can only see it with a partisan perspective.[16] My argument is that when Zizek locates lack and division in the Real, he is actually projecting a social and psychological conflict into reality, and therefore these antagonisms are rendered natural and inevitable. Instead of realizing that modern global human rights, democracy, and science are reliant on impartial reason, Zizek turns to a discredited ideology of Communism to resolve pressing threats like climate change, genetic manipulation, and refugees. Therefore, in the conclusion, I critique this return to Communism and offer the idea of Commonism as a better way to think about politics in a globalized world.

Notes

1. One of the challenging aspects in writing about Zizek's work is that he has written so much and has repeated himself so often that it is not always clear how to cite his work. Since I am focusing on his rhetoric, I will at times summarize repetitive trends in his work. I will also refer to the way he performs his work live, but there are few transcripts of his spoken speeches.
2. My work differs from other people who have used psychoanalysis to re-examine rhetoric because I focus on ethos, logos, pathos, and catharsis and not on metaphor, metonymy, and other tropes. For a different approach see Chaitin, Gilbert D. *Rhetoric and culture in Lacan*. Cambridge University Press, 1996.

3. Daniels, Charles B., and Sam Scully. "Pity, fear, and catharsis in Aristotle's Poetics." *Noûs* 26.2 (1992): 204–217.
4. Samuels, Robert. "The Pleasure Principle and the Death Drive." *Freud for the Twenty-First Century.* Palgrave Pivot, Cham, 2019. 17–25.
5. Freud, Sigmund. *Jokes and their relation to the unconscious.* WW Norton & Company, 1960.
6. Freud, Sigmund. *The psychopathology of everyday life.* WW Norton & Company, 1989.
7. By turning to catharsis, I differentiate my analysis from the approach made by Ernesto Laclau in *On Populist Reason.* Verso, 2005.
8. Žižek, Slavoj. *The sublime object of ideology.* Verso, 1989.
9. Jean Baudrillard makes a similar argument in *The Transparency of Evil,* Verso 1993.
10. Kwon, Min, et al. "Development and validation of a smartphone addiction scale (SAS)." *PloS one* 8.2 (2013): e56936.
11. Cole, Alyson Manda. *The cult of true victimhood: From the war on welfare to the war on terror.* Stanford University Press, 2007.
12. Aristotle, U. (2004). *Rhetoric.* Kessinger Publishing.
13. Fleming, Peter, and André Spicer. "Working at a cynical distance: Implications for power, subjectivity and resistance." *Organization* 10.1 (2003): 157–179.
14. Freud, Sigmund. "Formulations on the two principles of mental functioning." *The Standard Edition of the Complete Psychological Works of Sigmund Freud, Volume XII (1911–1913): The Case of Schreber, Papers on Technique and Other Works.* 1958. 213–226.
15. Samuels, Robert. *Freud for the Twenty-First Century: The Science of Everyday Life.* Springer, 2019.
16. Throughout this book, I capitalize Real, Symbolic, and Imaginary when I am referring to Lacan's definition of these terms.

CHAPTER 2

Catharsis: The Politics of Enjoyment

Abstract One of the first things that stands out about Zizek's discourse is his combination of high culture (philosophy) and low culture (popular culture). As an example of what many people call postmodernism, his work often uses humor to move beyond the modern divide between serious thought and entertainment. On one level, this combination of opposites points to the ways contemporary culture undermines past cultural distinctions by combining together multiple discourses. However, from a psychoanalytic rhetorical perspective, we should ask how does this use of language shape the meaning and effects of Zizek's writing and speaking? In other words, how is his discourse framed to direct the expectations of his audience? What matters then is not only what he says but what rhetorical mode frames his discourse.

Keywords Catharsis • Pleasure principle • Zizek • Aristotle • Trump • Postmodernism

One of the first things that stands out about Zizek's discourse is his combination of high culture (philosophy) and low culture (popular culture).[1] As an example of what many people call postmodernism, his work often uses humor to move beyond the modern divide between serious thought and entertainment.[2] On one level, this combination of opposites points to the ways contemporary culture undermines past cultural distinctions by

R. Samuels, *Zizek and the Rhetorical Unconscious*,
https://doi.org/10.1007/978-3-030-50910-1_2

combining together multiple discourses.[3] However, from a psychoanalytic rhetorical perspective, we should ask how does this use of language shape the meaning and effects of Zizek's writing and speaking? In other words, how is his discourse framed to direct the expectations of his audience? What matters then is not only what he says but what rhetorical mode frames his discourse.

It Begins with a Joke

To help clarify the role of catharsis in Zizek's work and contemporary culture, I will begin with an examination of a joke from his book *The Courage of Helplessness*:

> In my past work, I used a joke popular among dissidents from the good old days of "really-existing socialism". In fifteenth-century Russia, when it was occupied by Mongols, a farmer and his wife walk along a dusty country road. A Mongol warrior on horseback stops at their side and tells the farmer that he will now rape his wife. He then adds: "But, since there is a lot of dust on the ground, you should hold my testicles while I'm raping your wife, so that they will not get dirty!" After the Mongol finishes his job and rides away, the farmer starts to laugh and jump with joy. The surprised wife asks him: "How can you be jumping with joy when I was just brutally raped in your presence?" The farmer answers: "But I got him! His balls are full of dust!" This sad joke tells of the predicament of dissidents: they think they are dealing serious blows to the party nomenklatura, but all they are doing is getting a little bit of dust on the nomenklatura's testicles, while the nomenklatura continue raping the people. And can we not say exactly the same about Jon Stewart and co. making fun of Trump – do they not just dust his balls, or perhaps in the best of cases scratch them? (273)

This obscene joke is employed in part to question the use of humor in critiquing a political figure like Donald Trump, but what we should focus on is the way this example seeks to affect Zizek's audience. Not only is the joke obscene, insensitive, funny, and politically incorrect, but it also sets up a self-referential discourse.[4] In other words, Zizek is not just telling a joke, but he is reflecting on the use of humor in contemporary media culture and politics.

This self-referential representation of humor and popular culture serves many different functions: it tells us how we should respond to Zizek's own use of humor as it delivers pleasure to his audience by making a transgressive reference to rape. Part of the effect of this example is that it provokes the current Leftist investment in political correctness (PC) because it makes light of sexual violence. By taking a serious issue and putting it into an unserious context of humor, Zizek enacts a central aspect of our entertainment culture, which is the breaking down of the previous social divisions between high culture (theory) and low popular culture, the serious and the unserious, suffering and enjoyment, and fact and fiction. In getting us to laugh at his discussions of philosophy and politics, he brings together two opposed class cultures: on the one hand, we have the elitist academic analysis of society, and on the other hand, the "low-class" enjoyment of regressive humor. One of the results of this rhetoric is that a superficial overcoming of class conflict is achieved: an elite discourse bonds with the enjoyment of the anti-elite masses.

I first began to think about this strange combination of high theory and popular culture when I attended one of his lectures on Hegel, and I was surprised to hear so much laughter in the audience. Zizek himself kept saying that he was going to get to the serious philosophy soon, but he could not help himself from making a series of jokes. It was as if he was caught between two different relations with his audience: on one level he wanted to deliver new "serious" knowledge, but on another level, he wanted to keep them entertained.

To better understand Zizek's use of jokes, we can turn to Freud's theory of humor, which also tells us a lot about our contemporary entertainment culture.[5] Freud argued that there is an unspoken deal made between the joke teller and the audience: the speaker gives the audience pleasure, and in return, the audience promises not to hold the speaker responsible for what is said. Enjoyment here trumps responsibility and criticism, and so by framing a discourse around jokes, not only is the audience entertained, but one is able to say things that normally result in a critical response. As a form of catharsis, humor therefore fulfills the pleasure principle, which is founded on the drive to escape tension and conflict in order to use the least amount of mental energy as possible.[6] The bonding with the audience is then achieved through a circulation of enjoyment coupled with the removal of feelings of shame and guilt.

This misunderstood psychoanalytic theory of pleasure offers a key insight into how the unconscious functions in everyday life. Since societies are founded on the regulation of sex and violence, there is the necessity of producing a cultural space where these primal instincts can be enacted in a safe and accepted way.[7] When one tells a joke, not only does one often attack a person or idea, but one seduces the audience by giving them an unconscious form of pleasure. In this structure, one both laughs at the target (violence) and laughs with the audience (bonding).[8]

Zizek not only uses jokes and references to popular culture in order to bond with his audience, but also argues that all social structures are supported by a hidden form of obscene enjoyment.[9] For instance, the military not only functions through a system of commands and hierarchies, but the soldiers are constantly hazing each other and singing perverse songs and exchanging obscene jokes.[10] To understand the logic of these social structures, we have to acknowledge how the social law must also account for the desire to transgress the renunciation of instinctual impulses, and so a cultural safety valve needs to be provided.[11] We encounter this same theory expressed in Mikhail Bakhtin's notion of the carnivalesque: holidays and festivals provide an outlet for perverse, anti-social impulses in a contained manner; in fact, we can see much of popular culture today as enacting the formation of a safe space for the representation of violent and sexual tendencies in a displaced symbolic manner.[12] In terms of the framing of Zizek's own discourse, the turn to jokes, obscenities, and popular culture not only allow the audience to enjoy themselves in a safe, unconscious way, but everyone is able to escape from feelings of guilt and shame, yet, this escape must always fail, and the result is that negative feelings are repressed into the unconscious in the form of the irrational, demanding super-ego.[13]

It is therefore not sufficient to argue as Zizek has done throughout much of his work that the primary driving force behind culture and political ideology is enjoyment, since enjoyment does not fully account for the way that the pleasure principle relies on the combination of both a positive feeling and a process of denial. For instance, when people spend hours binge watching television shows, they are not just relaxing and enjoying themselves; they are also escaping the reality of their inner lives and the world around them.[14] Therefore, when entertainment becomes combined with politics, we can explain the popularity of specific politicians and ideologies based on the way they provide an avenue for escaping from dealing with pressing problems and conflicts, like climate change, racism, and economic inequality.

This theory of catharsis can help us to understand why Trump got so much free media attention during his campaign.[15] Since contemporary journalism is no longer shaped by the necessary but impossible modern ideal of discovering the truth in an objective manner, it has become just another form of capitalism and entertainment.[16] Moreover, due the fact that media outlets rely on gaining attention so that they can sell cable subscriptions and advertisements, they need to both attract an audience and sustain the audience's attention. While conflict and pathos can do the work of attracting the audience, there has to be something that keeps the audience engaged. Constant conflict would only produce a high level of anxiety and discomfort, and so it must be catharsis that sustains attention. However, it is not simply a question of flooding the brains of the audience with dopamine; rather, the real payoff is the escape from the self and the external social world.[17]

Catharsis and the Backlash of the Right

Evidence of the role of catharsis in the current world can be derived from understanding that the contemporary Right's primary project is not a defense of a more traditional past but a defense against feelings of guilt and shame. Not only does the Right define itself in opposition to the progressive Left, but it focuses its attention on how liberal culture tries to make people feel guilty for their aggressive thoughts and words; as a way of bringing together the upper class and the working class, this defense against shame and guilt shows how much of this coalition is held together through catharsis. Instead of addressing issues like climate change or economic inequality, the Right often focuses on looking for examples of extreme political correctness, and from this Right-wing perspective, the problem is not that people should feel guilty for destroying the environment and hording all of the resources; rather, the real problem is that the condescending Left wants to control us by making us feel bad for our thoughts and words.[18] In the Right's complaints about political correctness and identity politics, the underlying desire is to return to a mythical state where people were free to do and say what they wanted. To "Make America Great Again" points to the fantasy of a world before the Leftist super-ego.

To understand this aspect of neoliberalism, it is important to see how one of the main justifications for reducing taxes on the wealthy and big corporations in the United States is the idea that the only reason why we need these taxes is to pay for a bloated government, and what causes this excess is the high cost of welfare programs for poor people of color.[19] Of course, most people on welfare are white, and welfare programs make up a small part of the national budget; however, Reagan's idea of the "welfare queen" served the purpose of both demonizing poor people and representing the powerful as exploited and the exploited as the people with power.[20] Furthermore, an underlying idea was that since welfare programs were made to overcome prejudice and discrimination, in a post-prejudice society, these programs are no longer needed.[21] Part of the Right's agenda is then to deny racism and to blame claims of prejudice on the Left who has to invent racism in order to justify the liberal welfare state.[22] From this Right-wing perspective, identity politics and political correctness are derived from the imagination of liberals who want to take the money of the rich to fund unneeded welfare programs for the undeserving poor.

This twisted logic of the Right is largely unconscious and indirect, and so we need psychoanalysis to help us trace the use of rhetoric to manipulate the populace. For instance, one of the ironies of the Right declaring that we no longer have racism and discrimination in America is that their entire Republican Southern Strategy was centered on appealing to racist fears by talking about rising crime rates after the passage of the Civil Rights Act in 1964.[23] These politicians on the Right discovered that when they spoke about crime, their audience would associate criminal activity with black people, and so they were able to both appeal to racism and deny racism at the same time.[24] Here we see how in the structure of catharsis and the pleasure principle, the activation of desires is coupled with a denial of these same impulses.

Zizek and the Critique of Political Correctness

Of course, Trump is a master of appealing to racist fears in an indirect manner, but what makes his rhetoric truly cathartic is the way he will respond to criticism by simply attacking the people who are trying to make him feel guilty and ashamed for his words.[25] His sustained attacks on the "liberal media" are not only a way of rejecting the credibility of his critics, but he also uses this reaction to represent himself as a victim.[26] At times, we find this same employment of victim identity in Zizek's own rhetoric. For instance, in his debate with Jordan Peterson, he began with the following statement: "I cannot but notice the irony of how Peterson and I, the participants in this duel of the century, are both marginalized by the official academic community. I am supposed to defend here the left, liberal line against neo-conservatives. Really? Most of the attacks on me are now precisely from left liberals. Just remember the outcry against my critique of LGBT+ ideology, and I'm sure that if the leading figures in this field were to be asked if I were fit to stand for them, they would turn in their graves even if they are still alive."[27] Not only does Zizek represent himself as marginalized, but he follows the Right in focusing on how he has been a victim of attacks from the politically correct Liberal-Left for his controversial comments regarding transgender rights and other contentious issues.

Zizek may have made this comment to bond with Peterson, but he does have a long history of saying and writing things that he knows will provoke his Leftist critics. Although in the next chapter, I will also offer a criticism of some extreme forms of Leftist rhetoric, what I would like to examine here is the ways Zizek's discourse at times repeats the Right's backlash against postmodern social movements for equality. In looking at several passages from *Absolute Recoil,* I will examine the underlying unconscious rhetoric circulating in his discourse and the larger political culture.

The first example is focused on the Zizek's criticism of how the Left wants to use political correctness to censor how we speak and the intentions behind our speech acts:

> To prove the point, it suffices to recall the impasse of political correctness: the need for it arises when unwritten mores are no longer able to regulate everyday interactions effectively—in place of spontaneous customs followed in a non-reflexive way, we have explicit rules ("blacks" become "African Americans," "fat" becomes "weight-challenged," etc.). The main victim of such operations is precisely the order of "sincere lies," of pretense: under the discursive regime of political correctness, it is not enough to follow external rules of politeness, one is expected to be "sincerely" respectful of others, and continually examined on the sincerity of one's innermost convictions. In short, pushed to its extreme, the PC attitude resembles that of a proto- psychotic paranoid about the sincerity of every little politeness: greeting him with a "Hello, nice to meet you!," his reaction is: "Are you really glad to see me or are you just a hypocrite?" (61)

The key move in this argument is the jump from the desire of people to avoid discriminatory language to the claim that political correctness represents a paranoid suspicion of every statement.[28] Zizek's criticism here repeats the Right's strategy of transforming the desire to treat others with tolerance and fairness into an extremist form of censorship.[29] Of course, as we shall see in the next chapter, political correctness can go too far, but an underlying goal of the Left's political position is to fight against the use of social signifiers that belittle and debase different minority groups.

However, in the Right's effort to escape any guilt or responsibility for their speech, they turn themselves into the victims, while the people who are really being victimized are represented as the perpetrators.[30]

This reversal of victim and perpetrator in the fight against political correctness embodies several key unconscious rhetorical moves. First, one's aggression toward others is denied, and then this aggression is projected onto others who are seen as the true source of harm. This unconscious projection and denial is a central aspect of political catharsis because it allows the aggressor to escape from any sense of guilt or shame for the harm done by his or her words. This rhetoric also relies on exaggeration in order to make totalizing claims with little sense of proportion. For instance, in the following passage, Zizek uses hyperbole to mock the progressive social movements seeking to protect the rights of deaf people and other disadvantaged groups:

> The entire academic identity-politics machine is thus set in motion: scholars give courses and publish books on "deaf history" dealing with the oppression of the deaf and celebrating victims of Oralism, organize Deaf conventions, denounce speech therapists and hearing-aid manufacturers as a powerful lobby which wants to grind the deaf minority down, and so on and so forth. It is easy to make fun of this case—and one can imagine going several steps further: if Deaf Nation, why not Blind Nation, fighting the tyranny of Visualism? Why not Impotent and Frigid nation, oppressed by Sexualism? Why not the Fat Nation, terrorized by the health-food and the fitness lobbies? Why not Stupid Nation, brutally oppressed by the academic lobby? (591)

By moving from the need to protect deaf people to the protection of stupid and impotent people, Zizek uses exaggeration and humor to make light of actual serious social conflicts and acts of discrimination. Just as the Right uses extreme examples of political correctness to undermine the quest for equal treatment and the fight against hate speech, Zizek seeks to score political points by making fun of the progressive fight against discriminatory language use.

One of the ways that Zizek employs the unconscious political rhetoric of catharsis is through his use of humor, which is both exposed and reiterated in the following passage:

> Years ago, on the Santa Cruz campus, one of the capitals of Political Correctness, I was told that they had developed jokes which were funny

> without hurting, humiliating, or even making fun of anyone, like, "What happens when a triangle meets a circle? ... " Predictably, I immediately exploded: "I don't care what happens when a triangle meets a circle, the whole point of a joke is that there must be someone who gets hurt, humiliated ... !" (1011).

What is so telling in this example is the fact that Zizek thinks jokes can only be funny if they humiliate or hurt someone else. In other words, being offensive by going against political correctness and targeting specific minority groups is seen as a necessary part of humor and free speech.

For many people on the Right, free speech has suddenly become a major value because its celebration as a fundamental right can be used to demonize the Left's attempts at regulating hate speech and other forms of discriminatory discourse.[31] The Right has found that one way of drawing people's attention away from poverty and extreme economic inequality is to turn everyone's focus to cultural issues: thus, class warfare can be replaced by the culture wars so that the wealthy can protect their money and bond with the working class at the same time.[32] One reason, then, why Fox News and Donald Trump are so concerned about the attempts to regulate speech at universities is that they want to turn everyone's attention toward culture while they ignore issues of class, and they also need to continue to use hate speech to appeal to racist voters as they deny this appeal. By repressing both class conflict and the effects of hate speech, the Right provides the cathartic release of guilt, shame, and responsibility.

The Left and the Right are often locked into this culture war because both sides tend to see the world in terms of victims and perpetrators. We see an example of this rhetoric when Zizek states the following:

> This stance embodies the extreme version of the axiom of political correctness: we (white Western men) are ultimately responsible even when horrible things are done to us, so we should feel responsible for the perpetrator when he is punished – the perpetrator is not really an agent but a passive victim of circumstances, his crime is "a product of an unfair world, a product of an upbringing marked by war and despair" ... I consider this stance an exemplary case of perverse pathology: if taken seriously, it can be expanded indefinitely. Are we not all victims of circumstances and upbringing? (149–150)

Instead of judging individual cases of harm, Zizek ends up with the absurd universalizing claim that we are all victims. Driving this universalization of depravation is the borderline process of splitting: one is either an innocent victim or an evil perpetrator, while in reality, things are often much more complex and ambivalent.

One of the dangers in utilizing splitting, mirroring, denial, and projection is that one begins to lose the ability to make nuanced distinctions, and this lack of nuance feeds into our sound bite, polarized media culture as it tends to both represent extreme differences and erase these distinctions. In fact, we see this false equivalence between opposites in Zizek's equating of political correctness with religious fundamentalism: "at this level Left-liberal political correctness comes close to religious fundamentalism with its own list of 'impossible to remain silent when confronted with …': our own 'blasphemies' of (what is perceived as) sexism, racism, and other forms of intolerance" (164). The rhetoric here works by breaking down important differences as a universalizing claim is produced. First we have the equivalence between the Left and the religious Right, and then we also have the equivalence between the Left and liberals. The first problem is that the Left is often opposed to Christian fundamentalism, and the second issue is that liberals often reject the political correctness and identity politics of the Left. It appears that in Zizek's desire to dismiss the fight against "perceived" racism and sexism, he tries to persuade his audience by lumping three major political ideologies together and equating all of them with a fake fight against intolerance.

Another example of this same tendency to equate opposites and erase differences can be seen in his discussion of Islam:

> It is easy to mock the Islamic regulation of everyday life (a feature Islam shares with Judaism, incidentally), but what about the politically correct list of seduction moves that can be considered verbal harassment, of jokes that are considered racist or sexist or even "speciesist" (if one makes too much fun of other species of animals)? What one should emphasize here is the immanent contradiction of the Left-liberal stance: the libertarian stance of universal irony and mocking, making fun of all authorities, spiritual and political (the stance embodied in Charlie Hebdo), tends to slip into its opposite, an excessive sensitivity to the other's pain and humiliation. (164)

The first issue here is the loss of all proportion and distinction by equating Islamic law with the criticisms of sexist jokes. The next move is to somehow add libertarian ideology to the chain of equivalence running from Islamic fundamentalism to Left-Liberal political correctness: after all, the

Right has employed libertarian ideology in order to proclaim free speech as the ultimate liberty as it equates individual freedom to the free market.[33] In Zizek's case, it appears that these political terms are being used to persuade his audience that political correctness is the real thing they should fear.

One reason why Zizek cannot help but to repeat some of the worst parts of the Right's rhetoric is that he fundamentally rejects the modern liberal-democratic ideals of neutrality, compromise, rational negotiation, and mutual respect:

> Then there is the "reflexive" politically correct racism: the multiculturalist perception of Muslims as the terrain of ethnic horrors and intolerance, of primitive irrational war passions, to be opposed to the post-nation-state liberal-democratic process of solving conflicts through rational negotiations, compromises and mutual respect. Racism is here as it were elevated to the second power: it is attributed to the Other, while we occupy the convenient position of a neutral benevolent observer, righteously dismayed at the horrors going on down there. (165)

It will be my argument in the fifth chapter of this book that the modern ideals of neutrality and universality represent the driving forces behind global justice and psychoanalysis, but for now, it is important to stress how without a belief in the necessary but impossible ideal of neutrality, there can be no modern democracy or science.

While Zizek tends to reject the possibility of having a non-ideological and non-partisan perspective of the world, he does want to save humor and irony from political correctness: "further consequence of the PC attitude to speech is the spreading prohibition of irony: when one makes a remark considered non-PC, it is less and less possible to save oneself by claiming it was meant ironically" (194). As we shall see below, irony and humor are often used in order to shelter people from criticism since they can always say that their aggression was a joke, or it should not be taken too seriously.

Jokes and Catharsis

The use of humor creates an ironic discourse where one both says and unsays something.[34] For instance, when Zizek calls himself a Stalinist, are we supposed to take him seriously or are we supposed to understand that he is saying this in an ironic way, which places his words in imaginary scare quotes?[35] The answer to this question from the position of psychoanalytic rhetoric is that the irony allows two distinct messages to be presented at the same time. As Freud argued, when someone says that he was not thinking about his mother, we can be assured that on the unconscious level, he was thinking about his mother, and so negation is used to reveal a truth in a way where one cannot be held accountable.[36]

Irony and humor thus allow for an escape from responsibility, and as Sartre insisted, ethics rely on humans being both free and responsible.[37] What we then learn from the role of catharsis in our contemporary world is that we have an intense desire not to be responsible, and our use of rhetoric allows us to achieve this goal of catharsis through the satisfaction of the pleasure principle.[38] Even though this effort at catharsis always ultimately fails, it is behind much of our politics and culture today. For instance, one way of understanding Trump and his followers is to realize that much of his rhetoric concerns a desire to escape from any responsibility for what he says and does.[39] The main way that Trump achieves this goal is to blame others for what he is doing himself. For instance, he will attack a person, and then he will claim that he is being attacked. Likewise, his demonization of the media creates an ironic splitting because he is using the media to attack the media.[40]

Zizek's Ironic Discourse

From a psychoanalytic perspective, it is essential to see the relation between catharsis and irony. Since the person who makes an ironic statement signals that the words should not be taken at face value, the speaker is able to hold two different positions at the same time. For example, in the classic example of the liar's paradox, one is affirming that one is lying, but the audience does not know if the person is lying about lying.[41] Since the speaker cannot be held to one position, it is impossible to hold the speaker responsible for what is said. Not only does this help the speaker escape from any feelings of guilt and shame, but the audience is also put into the same ambivalent position.

Just as irony implies placing scare quotes around every statement, Zizek's entire discourse can be seen as enacting a doubling and distancing frame since once he employs humor and irony and combines serious philosophy with unserious jokes, there is no way to know for sure how to process what he is presenting. Moreover, this ironic structure shapes how he sees the way language works itself, and this conception of self-reflexivity applies to his own discourse. To further examine this use of irony, I will look at several passages from his book *For They Know Not What They Do: Enjoyment as a Political Factor*, where he makes the claim that all language is self-reflexive because language contains within itself a reference to its own failure to represent reality and subjectivity: [42] "The gap is not simply external to language, it is not a relationship between language and a subject external to it; rather, it is inscribed in the very heart of language in the guise of the irreducible (self) reflexivity" (xiii). Here, Zizek argues that the fundamental opposition between language and reality is part of the internal nature of language itself; in other words, language is internally divided, and so it must constantly try to hide this gap by referring to itself.

From this perspective, the way that language works is by constantly framing its own statements and then differentiating what it says from its attitude about what it is saying:

> When Lacan repeats that "there is no meta-language," this claim does not imply the impossibility of a reflexive distance towards some first-order language; on the contrary, "there is no meta-language" means, in fact, that there is no language – no seamless language whose enunciated is not broken by the reflexive inscription of the position of the enunciation. (xiii)

Zizek's argument appears to be that all language is always ironic and metafictional because the speaker has to constantly tell the audience how to interpret what is being said, and like the liar's paradox, a distinction is created between what one is saying and what one means to say.[43]

Zizek explains the self-division and self-reflexivity in language through the following problematic sexist example:

> Language, in its very notion, involves a minimal distance towards its literal meaning – not in the sense of some irreducible ambiguity or multiple dispersion of meanings, but in the more precise sense of "he said X, but what if he Really meant the opposite" – like the proverbial male-chauvinist notion of a woman who, when subjected to sexual advances, says, "No," while her real message is "Yes." (xiii)

Since people can lie and misrepresent what they are really thinking and intending, Zizek posits that it is important to distinguish between what one says (the statement) and what one really means (the enunciation).[44] In other terms, due the fact that we are often taking a subjective stance in relation to our own discourse, a divide may be opened up between our words and our true intentions. Yet, Zizek appears to take this particular linguistic issue and over-generalize it to the point that he claims that our intentions are always in conflict with what we say. Here an underlying desire to have a perfect match between intention and language results in the failure to see how in most instances, people do not feel separate from their own words.

Zizek not only wants to insist that language is always self-reflexive because the speaker has to take a stance on his or her own words, but more profoundly, language has to account for its inability to access the Real: "The self-reflexivity of language, the fact that a speech act is always a self-reflexive comment on itself… bears witness to the impossibility inscribed into the very heart of language: its failure to grasp the Real" (xiv). Since we only can know about truth through language, and language does not necessarily relate to reality, Zizek affirms that the Symbolic order of language cannot access the Real.[45] Language then tries to cover up for its failure to refer to reality by referring to itself instead. This theory can help us to understand how in a culture that is full of media referring to other media, the goal is to represent representations and not reality itself.[46]

In the case of Zizek's own discourse, self-reflexivity means the distinctions between truth and fiction, the serious and the unserious, and language and reality break down. Not only does this loss of cultural differences make it hard to analyze his work or to know what he is actually trying to say, but it allows him to critique the world as he retains a self-reflexive distance from his own words.

Trump, Zizek, and Reality Media

My goal here is not to say that Zizek is just like Trump or that he is a Right-wing thinker; rather, I want to show how an aspect of his rhetoric that frames his discourse entails an ironic splitting that we also find in Trump and contemporary media culture. Since he posits that the conflict between the Symbolic and the Real is contained within the Symbolic itself, he not only eliminates a central distinction of psychoanalysis, but also posits that the failures of language can be resolved through language. In a similar vein, reality media is based on the notion that Symbolic media can be made Real by its self-referential relation to itself. As a response to scripted media, what many people find attractive about reality media is that it uses real people in real situations so that the fakeness of its representations are overcome through the authenticity and im-mediacy of its performance.[47] As Gilbert Chaitin argues in *Rhetoric & Culture in Lacan*, in the performance of a speech act, the distinctions between words and intentions and representation and reality are lost since one creates a new reality through a self-reflexive gesture; however, the ultimate effect of this use of language is the production of non-sense (66). Furthermore, what some people like about Trump is that he is supposed to be real and authentic because he refuses to be censored or scripted. So even if Trump is telling a lie, his supporters think that he is being truthful because he says whatever is on his mind without a filter. This authenticity allows a billionaire to bond with the working class because they see him as different from the other fake establishment politicians.[48]

Trump's cynical use of irony to bond with the masses can be seen in a series of statements he made during a campaign rally in 2019. In analyzing his words, I want to examine how his rhetoric delivers catharsis to his audience by suspending any sense of accountability.[49] The first example relates to the idea that due to political correctness and the need to be sensitive to other cultures and religions, Americans stopped being able to talk about Christmas in public: "And did you notice that everybody is saying merry Christmas again? Did you notice?" On one level, this is an incredibly trivial thing for a president to say, but what he is appealing to is the idea that before he came into office, people were having their daily language censored. Of course, there is no way of knowing if more people are actually feeling free to say "Merry Christmas," but what matters is that Trump is presenting himself as the champion of people who think they are being controlled by the Leftist PC police. His rhetoric also has the added bonus of signaling to his Christian supporters that he is not concerned with recognizing or protecting other religions.

This fight against political correctness is continued in the next statement, which is referring to the way security guards were removing a protester from his rally: "I don't know who the security company is, but the police came up but they want to be so politically correct. So they don't grab her wrists lightly and get her out. They say, oh would you please come – would you please come with me?" The hidden idea in this complaint against the politically correct security people is that in the old days, the police were much more violent and aggressive, but now, they have to be gentle with the people they are handling. Trump is not directly telling the security guards to be more violent, but he is signaling to his audience that if he had his way, protesters would be treated in much more violent way.[50] This indirect, ironic discourse tells his audience that not only is the PC culture making it hard for the police to do their job, but Trump himself prefers a much more violent reaction. However, the way he presents his words makes it hard to claim that he is directly inciting violence, and thus he is both saying and not saying the same thing in an ironic, cathartic manner.

Of course, Trump's constant references to political correctness uses "dog whistles" to communicate to his supporters in an unconscious way.[51] We see this type of irony in the following statement: "See, in the old days – in the old days I would say mankind, now I say mankind, womankind. This way I don't get in trouble with our friends." Trump is mocking gender-neutral language by referring to the good old days when people did not have to worry about offending women. Yet, in the way he presents his words, he signals that he is both being censored and refusing to be censored at the same time.

Trump's ironic double-speak often reaches its peak when he refers to the media.[52] On the one hand, he needs the media in order to get attention, but he also feels the media treats him unfairly, and so he constantly refers to the fact that he is being filmed while he attacks the media itself: "The cameras – do you ever notice I go to these stadiums, 25–30,000 people. They never show the crowd." As a television performer, Trump is obsessed about getting screen time and being at the center of everyone's attention, and yet, he also feels that the media under-reports the size of his audiences.[53] Unlike politicians from the past, who would never comment on the fact that they are being filmed, as a reality media star, Trump breaks the fourth wall and directly makes the invisible camera present. One of the effects of this gesture is to show that the media determines everything, and there is no difference between a real person and a performer.[54] Moreover, since he wants to satisfy the audience that feels the media is part of the PC liberal establishment, he also has to attack the media while he demands more attention. The end result is that he constantly gets free publicity as the media spirals into a self-reflexive analysis concerning how Trump attacks them.

Of course, a central part of Trump's rhetoric is his constant exaggerations, which make it hard to tell what he really thinks because what he says is so disconnected from actual reality.[55] In the next example, we see him returning to his obsession about having a large audience: "I don't think we've ever had an empty seat from the time I came down the escalator.

That's a long time ago. I don't think we've ever had an empty seat." Of course, his claim that he has never had an empty seat at one of his rallies is contradicted by the empty seats at the present rally, but he does not seem to be concerned with how his words match up to reality. As a performer, he seeks to produce the reality that he describes through a self-reflexive discourse that makes constant references to his audience, the media, and his own words.[56]

Trump's basic amoral opportunism not only allows him to say whatever pops into his head, but he also tends to contradict himself without any concern.[57] For instance, in the following statement concerning another politician, he signals to his audience that he is not supposed to say what he is thinking, but he just can't help himself from doing it: "He walks up to the mics, I mean, we're not – and no offense, I don't want to be – because with me too I never think about looks anymore. OK. I don't talk about looks of a male or female but in his case let's just say, last time I'll ever refer to this. He's not exactly the best-looking guy we've ever seen." The fact that a president is saying any of this in public is shocking, but that is part of his appeal; he knows that he should be controlling his aggressive impulses, but he just can't contain himself, and this lack of impulse control tells his audience that maybe they shouldn't regulate their impulses either.[58]

If there was any doubt that Trump does not differentiate between politics and entertainment, the following statement should make it clear that he has fully embraced the fusing of art, politics, and business: "[Democrats will] receive a big backlash at the box office." Not only does he see the other political party as a movie trying to sell more tickets, but he uses the term backlash to appropriate the criticism of his own reactionary discourse.[59] This spread of entertainment to all aspects of our lives forces us to question whether things can ever go back to "normal?"

In perhaps Trump's most revealing ironic self-reflection, he claims that due to the scrutiny of a media system that hates him, he always has to tell the truth: "I have to be always very truthful because if I'm a little bit off they call me a liar." Like the liar's paradox, it is unclear if he is saying that he always tells the truth, or if he is saying that even when he only lies a little, he is called a liar. Perhaps, it does not matter to his followers if his words do not fit reality because like a television show, he quickly moves on to the next thing after he constructs a false reality for them.

In a public form of wild free association, Trump's desire to be authentic and not be censored pushes him to speak in a fragmented and incoherent manner. This lack of prepared speech is apparent in the next statement: "You know, you're the elite. They're not the elite. You're the elite. You're the elite. You do better than they do. They talk about – don't you hate it – well (ph) the elite. Oh, really? I went to better schools. Many of you went to better schools. We won't talk about homes even though your homes are nice here." It appears that Trump is trying to say here that the elites are not really the elites, and the people in his audience who are looked down on by the elites are the real elites. Of course, he has to mention that he went to better schools than the supposed elites, and here he reveals himself as really being part of the elite establishment, but due to the fluid nature of his rhetoric, he is able to both reverse the meaning of elite as he represents himself as both an elite and part of the anti-elite masses.

Trump the Primal Father

It should be clear from the above statements that what many of his followers like about him is that they see him as being real and authentic because he refuses to be controlled by the politically correct thought police. From a psychoanalytic perspective, we can say that Trump represents the fantasy of the primal father who has total freedom and direct access to enjoyment without any social restrictions.[60] Here we find the myth of the perverse father who avoids the censoring super-ego and is able to act directly on his instinctual impulses.

The fundamental fantasy of the primal father also affects the notions of free speech, the free market, and the free individual shaping much of Right-wing ideology. What often unites the Right is the idea that they are being victimized because they are unable to say or do what they want.[61] According to this fantasy structure, the cause of the loss of primal freedom is the liberal super-ego, which tries to make them feel guilty and ashamed for their thoughts and speech. Thus the Right-wing media constantly finds examples of the censoring of speech in order to show how the liberal media and university culture is the perpetrator of repression.[62] In this vicious loop, the Right uses hate speech to provoke a reaction by the liberal culture, which then is used to place the Right in the position of the victim and not the perpetrator. As a victim and primal father, Trump caters to both sides of this fantasy structure: on one side, he is the subject barred by the censoring Symbolic order, and on the other side, he represents the one who has total access to unlimited freedom and Real enjoyment.

When Trump said that when you are rich and famous, you can grab women anywhere you want, he was re-stating the Marquis de Sade's idea that he has a right to enjoy any part of any person.[63] As the primal father, Trump is seen as being free to enjoy, and his followers identify with this perverse freedom. Moreover, as a former reality TV star, Trump's rise to power points to the ways contemporary culture seeks to provide access to immediate pleasure in an unscripted manner.[64] Not only do Trump's supporters believe that Trump is the most honest president ever because he says whatever he thinks, but they suspend their own reality-testing in their hypnotic relation to his rhetoric.[65] In turn, Trump himself appears to parrot what he hears on Fox News, and so an information-entertainment entity serves to frame his discourse and the reception of his audience.[66]

Technologies of Catharsis

It is vital to understand the role of technology in our entertainment culture of catharsis because new devices like the iPhone deliver instant pleasure to its users in an intoxicating manner.[67] By following Freud's idea that pleasure actually entails the escape from tension and stimulation, we can comprehend that what makes these media devices so addicting is that they allow a person to erase their own subjectivity.[68] As an escape from tension and responsibility, we turn to media technologies to derive an autistic and autoerotic enjoyment, which removes social mediation and the desire of others from our interactions. For instance, I once asked a student why she was always on her phone during class, and she said she takes out this device whenever she is feeling anxious. I then asked her what makes her feel anxious, and she replied the ideas of others.

Freud writes in *Civilization and Its Discontents*, "The service rendered by intoxicating media in the struggle for happiness and in keeping misery at a distance is so highly prized as a benefit that individuals and people alike have given them an established place in the economics of the libido. We owe to such media not merely the immediate yield of pleasure, but also a greatly desired degree of independence from the external world" (25).[69] Freud, here, was talking about narcotics, but he also could have been referring to mass media in the age of binge watching and virtual reality. While the immersion in streaming media can keep misery at a distance, as it provides an immediate pleasure, it also functions to deny reality and prevent the difficult task of improving the world and addressing personal conflicts.[70]

For Freud, the state of hypnosis is equated with passionate love and the submission to the group because in all of these cases, the subject is returned to the position of a helpless child in front of an all-powerful primal father.[71] In terms of contemporary media, the suspension of disbelief in the process of immersion serves to disable the reality principle and leads to the pure culture of the pleasure principle and catharsis. From this perspective, the biggest threat to humankind might be the retreat from reality through pleasure.[72]

Although Zizek does not focus on the pleasure principle, he follows Lacan in the usage of the term "jouissance," which is often translated as enjoyment.[73] In French, the main meaning of this word is orgasm, and as Zizek argues, Lacan's work can be divided into an early period where he emphasizes desire and Symbolic castration and a later period, where attention is centered on jouissance and the Real.[74] The problem with this binary reading of Lacan's work is that it can be read as privileging enjoyment as the goal of analysis. However, the end of analysis requires a confrontation with the fundamental conflicts between pleasure and reality, sexuality and the law, the Real and the Symbolic, nature and culture, and the individual and society. These unresolvable oppositions are hidden by the pursuit of enjoyment, which uses catharsis to escape from the reality principle.

Instead of utilizing Freud's theory of the reality principle, Zizek follows the later Lacan in stressing the concept of the Real as that which is impossible to Symbolize. However, Lacan insists that nothing lacks in the Real, and our sense of loss is only possible because we have Symbolic markers that can be missing.[75] Zizek will reverse this logic by locating lack in the Real.[76] For instance, he argues that quantum mechanics shows how reality and nature are themselves incomplete; in other words, he projects Symbolic loss into the Real.[77] One of the effects of this displacement is that the fault is not in ourselves but exists in nature. We can understand this move through the notion that societies produce their own contained outside in order to create the illusion of freedom, enjoyment, and realness. From this perspective, nature, sex, and authenticity are symbolic objects created by social systems so that they can control rebellion and desire.[78]

As we see in Right-wing libertarian politics, the desired freedom from Symbolic social law is coupled with a freedom to pursue pleasure as a fundamental right. It is therefore the fantasy of uncivilized freedom and enjoyment that powers the conservative counter-revolution. I have argued that Zizek's use of catharsis and his privileging of enjoyment unintentionally replicates aspects of this Right-wing discourse. In the next chapter, we shall see how the Right's use of catharsis can be opposed to the Left's employment of pathos.

Notes

1. Mendible, Myra. "High theory/low culture: Postmodernism and the politics of carnival." *Journal of American Culture* 22.2 (1999): 71–76.
2. Mendible, Myra. "High theory/low culture: Postmodernism and the politics of carnival." *Journal of American Culture* 22.2 (1999): 71–76.
3. Samuels, Robert. "Auto-modernity after postmodernism: Autonomy and automation in culture, technology, and education." *Digital youth, innovation, and the unexpected* (2008).
4. Lucca, Violet. "NO JOKE." *Film Comment* 53.2 (2017): 52.
5. Freud, Sigmund. "Jokes and their Relation to the Unconscious." *The Standard Edition of the Complete Psychological Works of Sigmund Freud, Volume VIII (1905): Jokes and their Relation to the Unconscious.* 1960. 1–247.
6. Freud, Sigmund. "Project for a scientific psychology (1950 [1895])." *The Standard Edition of the Complete Psychological Works of Sigmund Freud, Volume I (1886–1899): Pre-Psycho-Analytic Publications and Unpublished Drafts.* 1966. 281–391.
7. Bakhtin, Mikhail Mikhaĭlovich, and Mikhail Bakhtin. *Rabelais and his world.* Vol. 341. Indiana University Press, 1984.
8. Samuels, Robert. "The Political without Politics: Slavoj Zizek and the Psychoanalysis of Automodernity." *New Media, Cultural Studies, and Critical Theory after Postmodernism.* Palgrave Macmillan, New York, 2009. 69–83.
9. Žižek, Slavoj. *The plague of fantasies.* Verso, 1997.
10. Zizek, Slavoj, and Glyn Daly. *Conversations with Zizek.* John Wiley & Sons, 2013.
11. Liu, Alan Y. "The power of formalism: the new historicism." (1989): 721–771.
12. Bakhtin, Mikhail. "25□ Carnival and the Carnivalesque." *Cultural theory and popular culture: A reader* (1997): 250.
13. Freud, Sigmund. "The ego and the id (1923)." *TACD Journal* 17.1 (1989): 5–22.
14. Panda, Swati, and Satyendra C. Pandey. "Binge watching and college students: Motivations and outcomes." *Young Consumers* 18.4 (2017): 425–438.
15. Pickard, Victor. "Media failures in the age of Trump." *The Political Economy of Communication* 4.2 (2017).
16. Boorstin, Daniel Joseph. *The image: A guide to pseudo-events in America.* Vintage, 1992.
17. Kwon, Jung-Hye, Chung-Suk Chung, and Jung Lee. "The effects of escape from self and interpersonal relationship on the pathological use of

Internet games." *Community Mental Health Journal* 47.1 (2011): 113–121.
18. Flanagan, Scott C., and Aie-Rie Lee. "The new politics, culture wars, and the authoritarian-libertarian value change in advanced industrial democracies." *Comparative Political Studies* 36.3 (2003): 235–270.
19. Palley, Thomas I. "From Keynesianism to neoliberalism: Shifting paradigms in economics." *Neoliberalism: A critical reader* April (2005): 20–29.
20. Hancock, Ange-Marie. *The politics of disgust: The public identity of the welfare queen.* NYU Press, 2004.
21. Samuels, Robert. "The Political without Politics: Slavoj Zizek and the Psychoanalysis of Automodernity." *New Media, Cultural Studies, and Critical Theory after Postmodernism.* Palgrave Macmillan, New York, 2009. 69–83.
22. d'Souza, Dinesh. *Illiberal education: The politics of race and sex on campus.* Simon and Schuster, 1991.
23. Aistrup, Joseph A. *The southern strategy revisited: Republican top-down advancement in the South.* University Press of Kentucky, 2015.
24. Tonry, Michael. "The social, psychological, and political causes of racial disparities in the American criminal justice system." *Crime and Justice* 39.1 (2010): 273–312.
25. Schneider, Andrea Kupfer. "Negotiating from the bully pulpit: Teaching Trump, tactics, and turmoil." *Negotiation Journal* 35.1 (2019): 19–01.
26. Ioanide, Paula. *The emotional politics of racism: How feelings trump facts in an era of colorblindness.* Stanford University Press, 2015.
27. A transcript of this debate can be found at: https://docs.google.com/document/d/1rUhYdqB2Jh7CU5Le0XgktKaoXQmnTdbv0-_kE5BQL6Q/edit
28. Wilson, John K. *The myth of political correctness: The conservative attack on higher education.* Duke University Press, 1995.
29. Fairclough, Norman. "Political correctness': The politics of culture and language." *Discourse & Society* 14.1 (2003): 17–28.
30. Norton, Michael I., and Samuel R. Sommers. "Whites see racism as a zero-sum game that they are now losing." *Perspectives on Psychological Science* 6.3 (2011): 215–218.
31. Talbot, Mary. "Political correctness and freedom of speech." *Hellinger et al* (2007): 751–764.
32. Giroux, Henry. "Authoritarianism, Class Warfare, and the Advance of Neoliberal Austerity Policies." *Knowledge Cultures* 5.1 (2017): 13–20.
33. Freeman, Samuel. "Illiberal libertarians: Why libertarianism is not a liberal view." *Philosophy & Public Affairs* 30.2 (2001): 105–151.

34. Magill, R. Jay. *Chic ironic bitterness.* University of Michigan Press, 2007.
35. Galt Harpham, Geoffrey. "Doing the impossible: Slavoj Žižek and the end of knowledge." *Critical Inquiry* 29.3 (2003): 453–485.
36. Freud, Sigmund. "Negation." *International Journal of Psycho-Analysis* 6 (1925): 367–371.
37. Sartre, Jean-Paul. *Being and nothingness: An essay in phenomenological ontology.* Citadel Press, 2001.
38. Fromm, Erich. *Escape from freedom.* Macmillan, 1994.
39. McComiskey, Bruce. *Post-truth rhetoric and composition.* University Press of Colorado, 2017.
40. Perkins, Robert L., ed. *The concept of Irony.* Vol. 2. Mercer University Press, 2001.
41. Parsons, Terence. "Assertion, denial, and the liar paradox." *Journal of Philosophical Logic* (1984): 137–152.
42. Žižek, Slavoj. *For they know not what they do: Enjoyment as a political factor.* Verso, 2002.
43. Hutcheon, Linda. "Beginning to theorize postmodernism." *Textual Practice* 1.1 (1987): 10–31.
44. Sulkunen, Pekka, and Jukka Törrönen. "Constructing speaker images: The problem of enunciation in discourse analysis." *Semiotica* 115.1–2 (1997): 121–146.
45. Glynos, Jason, and Yannis Stavrakakis. "Encounters of the real kind." *Laclau: A critical reader* (2004): 201–16.
46. Baudrillard, Jean. *Simulacra and simulation.* University of Michigan Press, 19.
47. Holmes, Su, and Deborah Jermyn, eds. *Understanding reality television.* Psychology Press, 2004.
48. Frank, Thomas. *Pity the billionaire: The hard-times swindle and the unlikely comeback of the right.* Macmillan, 2012.
49. The Transcript of Trump's speech can be found at: https://www.cnn.com/2019/12/19/politics/donald-trump-michigan-rally-impeachment/index.html
50. Giroux, Henry A. "White nationalism, armed culture and state violence in the age of Donald Trump." *Philosophy & Social Criticism* 43.9 (2017): 887–910.
51. Goldstein, Donna M., and Kira Hall. "Postelection surrealism and nostalgic racism in the hands of Donald Trump." *HAU: Journal of Ethnographic Theory* 7.1 (2017): 397–406.
52. Kellner, Douglas. "Donald Trump, Media Spectacle, and Authoritarian Populism." *Fast Capitalism* 14.1 (2019).

53. Kristiansen, Lars J., and Bernd Kaussler. "The Bullshit Doctrine: Fabrications, Lies, and Nonsense in the Age of Trump." *Informal Logic* 38.1 (2018): 13–52.
54. Postman, Neil. *Amusing ourselves to death: Public discourse in the age of show business*. Penguin, 2006.
55. Boczkowski, Pablo J., and Zizi Papacharissi, eds. *Trump and the media*. MIT Press, 2018.
56. Kakutani, Michiko. *The death of truth*. Tim Duggan Books, 2019.
57. Kellner, Douglas. "Donald Trump as authoritarian populist: A Frommian analysis." (2016).
58. Gopnik, Adam. "The dangerous acceptance of Donald Trump." *The New Yorker* (2016).
59. Douthat, Ross. "Trump hacked the media right before our eyes." *New York Times* (2018).
60. Adorno, Theodor W. "Freudian theory and the pattern of fascist propaganda." *DERS. (Hrsg.). Gesammelte Schriften Bd* 8 (1951): 408–433.
61. Samuels, Robert. *Psychoanalyzing the Left and Right After Donald Trump: Conservatism, Liberalism, and Neoliberal Populisms*. Springer, 2016.
62. Horowitz, David. *David Horowitz*. University of Wisconsin-Madison, 2001.
63. Lacan, Jacques, and James B. Swenson. "Kant with Sade." *October* 51 (1989): 55–75.
64. Haralovich, Mary Beth, and Michael W. Trosset. *"Expect the Unexpected": narrative pleasure and uncertainty due to chance in survivor*. na, 2004.
65. Dubrofsky, Rachel E. "Authentic Trump: yearning for civility." *Television & New Media* 17.7 (2016): 663–666.
66. Flaxman, Seth, Sharad Goel, and Justin M. Rao. "Filter bubbles, echo chambers, and online news consumption." *Public opinion quarterly* 80 S1 (2016): 298–320.
67. Lindstrom, Martin. "You love your iPhone. Literally." *New York Times* 1 (2011): 21A.
68. Lindstrom, Martin. "You love your iPhone. Literally." *New York Times* 1 (2011): 21A.
69. Freud, Sigmund. *Civilization and its discontents*. Broadview Press, 2015.
70. Bainbridge, Caroline. "Box-set mind-set: Psycho-cultural approaches to binge watching, gender, and digital experience." *Free Associations* 75 (2019): 65–83.
71. Freud, Sigmund. *Group Psychology and the Analysis of the Ego*. Penguin UK, 2004.
72. Baudrillard, Jean. *The transparency of evil: Essays on extreme phenomena*. Verso, 1993.
73. Gallop, Jane. "Beyond the Jouissance principle." *Representations* 7 (1984): 110–115.

74. Žižek, Slavoj. *Enjoy your symptom!: Jacques Lacan in Hollywood and out.* Routledge, 2013.
75. Julien, Philippe. *Jacques Lacan's return to Freud: the real, the symbolic, and the imaginary.* NYU Press, 1995.
76. See Chap. 4 of the present work.
77. Zizek, Slavoj. "Lacan with quantum physics." *FutureNatural: Nature, Science, Culture* (1996): 270–89.
78. Grady, Hugh. "Containment, subversion—and postmodernism." *Textual Practice* 7.1 (1993): 31–49.

CHAPTER 3

Pathos, Hysteria, and the Left

Abstract The psychoanalytic theory of emotion must be understood through the workings of the primary processes in the unconscious. Since affects are displaced while one event is substituted for another event, we see how the rhetorical figures of metaphor (substitution) and displacement (metonymy) determine how emotions are produced in the unconscious. Freud added that these processes occur in an automatic fashion and do not rely on the intentionality of the subject; moreover, these primary processes fail to differentiate between fact and fiction, and so they make fantasies, hallucinations, and imagination possible. From a rhetorical perspective, pathos as emotion is opposed to reason and logos.

Keywords Emotion • Pathos • Hysteria • Freud • Zizek • Unconscious • Left-wing

In the previous chapter, I stressed how catharsis represents the pleasure principle's drive to escape tension and conflict. For Aristotle, this mode of rhetoric is based on the purgation of feelings of pity and fear.[1] Thus, from his perspective, one goes to the theater in order to experience a set of emotions that are then released and removed by the end of the production. Of course, Freud called his initial form of psychoanalytic treatment catharsis because the goal was to remove symptoms by restoring repressed memories.[2] This technique was originally developed through his work

R. Samuels, *Zizek and the Rhetorical Unconscious*,
https://doi.org/10.1007/978-3-030-50910-1_3

with hysterical patients, who he argued suffered from intense emotions that did not seem to have a clear cause. In fact, he reasoned that the emotions of these patients did not make sense because they were derived from the displacement of one memory onto another memory.[3] According to this logic of the unconscious, an original traumatic event was repressed and replaced by another related event, and so the hysteric experienced an emotional reaction to the second event and not the first event. The goal then of catharsis was to discover the original cause of the emotion so that it could be released.[4] Here we see the fundamental conflict between pathos and catharsis, since the goal of catharsis is to release pathos.

The psychoanalytic theory of emotion must be understood through the workings of the primary processes in the unconscious. Since affects are displaced while one event is substituted for another event, we see how the rhetorical figures of metaphor (substitution) and displacement (metonymy) determine how emotions are produced in the unconscious.[5] Freud added that these processes occur in an automatic fashion and do not rely on the intentionality of the subject; moreover, these primary processes fail to differentiate between fact and fiction, and so they make fantasies, hallucinations, and imagination possible.[6]

This theory of unconscious pathos plays a central role in politics today because it helps us to understand the ways social movements on the Left and the Right use emotion to create group solidarity through the formation of hysterical identifications and a victim-based fantasy structure.[7] In the case of examining progressive social movements, the psychoanalysis of unconscious political rhetoric reveals how these movement are often based on a founding trauma, and this traumatic exploitation or violence generates a structure where people identify with a shared sense of victimization. My goal here is not to deny the real suffering and exploitation of people; rather psychoanalysis forces us to ask what role does victimhood play in the formations of identities and identifications?[8]

In the previous chapter, I focused on the use of victim politics on the Right, but in this chapter, I want to look at how the pathos of victim identification helps to structure social movement on the Left for better and worse. I believe this analysis can help us to understand why the Right seems to have little problem forming a coalition among middle-class Christian fundamentalists, wealthy libertarians, and the working-class, but the Left is often fragmented by the competition among different identity groups. One possible explanation for this distinction is that the victim identities of the Right are derived mostly from imaginary fantasies, while the Left seeks to organize people who have been really victimized by race, gender, and class hierarchies.[9] Since these real structural victimizations and exploitations are so traumatic and emotionally charged, each victimized group has a hard time sacrificing their suffering to focus on the victimization of other exploited groups. It is as if one has to choose between sexism, racism, and classism when one is joining a political group on the Left.[10]

In the case of Zizek's work, the central traumatic cause is global capitalism in the form of class struggle and exploitation.[11] Although he does at times discuss issues concerning racism and sexism, it is clear that his perspective is focused on capitalism as the central cause of human suffering. Like many academic thinkers and politicians on the Left, what his work does not do is show how racism, sexism, and class conflict are part of the same unconscious social structure. It is vital to stress that premodern cultures are shaped by sexist and racist hierarchies, and therefore, these systems of oppression pre-exist modern capitalism. In fact, Marx argues that capitalism melts away all premodern traditions, beliefs, and borders; therefore, modernity and its extension through globalization can be understood as the potential undermining of premodern prejudices.[12]

This conflict between premodern patriarchy and modernity is one of the sources for postmodern hysterical subjectivity and social movements on the Left. Fundamentally, social movements seeking to expand the rights of oppressed minority groups are demanding an expansion of modern universal democratic law.[13] Furthermore, we can read hysterical symptoms as a mode of protest and complaint pointing to the trauma caused by the continual existence of premodern hierarchies and systems of exploitation. On the level of the individual, hysterical symptoms represent a resistance to the discourse of the master as embodied by the paternal Symbolic order within the Oedipus complex.[14] This hysteric structure is an unconscious formation because it functions in an automatic and unintentional manner, and it does not necessarily distinguish between real and fictional representations. Furthermore, as Freud showed in *Mass Psychology and the Analysis of the Ego*, hysterical emotions spread easily through identification and empathy; for instance, he gives the example of a girl in a boarding house receiving a letter from her lost lover, and all of the other girls cry along with her. Freud posited that hysterical identification occurs on the level of placing oneself in the same position as the suffering victim (48–49).

From a social perspective, empathy and identification are necessary to the formation of a group, and this reliance on an emotional bond reveals the role played by pathos. People bond with the suffering of others and share the same emotional state because emotions are first learned by the infant copying the reactions of others.[15] Emotions are thus learned behavior generated through imitation, and this makes them prone to be overwhelming and contagious. The paradox of social movements is that they need pathos in order to motivate and connect people, but this reliance on emotion can block the broader goal of being included into the impersonal universal law; moreover, a reliance on emotional contagion suspends the realty principle and makes these groups prone to irrational thinking and extreme behavior.[16]

I first began to understand this connection between hysteria and the Left during a time when my faculty union was taken over by a group of people who no longer believed in the need to negotiate with the administration. Our organization began to function like a cult with a charismatic leader who no one would question even when she said things that had not apparent connection to reality. Her basic strategy was to argue that we are innocent victims of an evil regime, and therefore no compromise was possible. In order to rally her base, she would exaggerate the state of their oppression and would feed on their desire for a utopian solution.

Around the same time, I became very involved in the presidential campaign of Bernie Sanders. One of the things that struck me the most about this experience was the way that people at his rallies would act as if they were at a rock concert or a religious revival meeting. When I tried to ask them which policies they endorsed and why, they usually had no clear response, but they were taken by the antagonistic splitting between the good "us" and the evil "them" (Republicans, the 1%, the liberal establishment, corporations). I also found that Sanders himself was not open to any criticism or change in his arguments, even when reality was clearly at odds with what he was saying. For instance, throughout the campaign, he would call for a revolution, but when people asked him what that revolution would entail, he had no real response.

Although we need postmodern social movements to expand the modern universal law of equal treatment, these movements can become fixated on pathos, identity, and identification. Thus, a problem then with contemporary identity politics is that it can be highly sectarian, divisive, and irrational because it is reliant on unconscious processes.[17] From a psychoanalytic rhetorical perspective, identity groups create solidarity by drawing a strict line between the good "us" and the "evil" them. This antagonistic logic is dependent on the binary structure of language where one signifier is differentiated from other signifiers. One of the results of this unconscious linguistic system is that the perception of the self and the other becomes split into extremes, and this splitting leads to the formation of victim identity and identification.[18]

Since the victim is always innocent, the other is blamed for all problems. Furthermore, the vengeance of the victim is justified, and one cannot criticize the victim. When a social group takes on this fantasy structure, reality-testing is suspended, since you cannot question or critique the suffering of the victim. In terms of psychological development, the original cause for this fantasy is the role of the paternal function in separating the infant from the mother.[19] As an embodiment of the premodern social order, the father has to threaten the child with castration or some other act of violence in order to motivate the child to freely choose to give up the original source of satisfaction and emotional bonding.[20] While the role of the mother and father are Symbolic and not necessarily based on the real sexual identity of the parents, the fundamental logic linking social and individual development requires the intervention of a third term separating the dual relation between the subject and the primary object.[21] Hysteria, is then, in part, derived from the protest against this intervention, which has a historical and personal side.[22]

In terms of contemporary culture, we are experiencing a global move away from premodern patriarchy, and part of this revolution has been caused by the protests and complaints of women who have used their bodies and voices to display their resistance to the oppressive sexual hierarchy. Like the rebellion of slaves, women realize that as an oppressed group, their power often is derived from their ability to stop working for the master.[23] Hysterical symptoms can be read in this way as a personal strike and a protest against abuse and exploitation.[24] However, since the disempowered class does not have the same power and tools as the dominant class, it often becomes necessary for the oppressed to use their bodies as the means for protest and resistance. In the case of hysteria, we see how the symptoms are usually manifested in bodily discomfort and discontinuities. For instance, Freud argued that when a hysteric suddenly loses her ability to walk, this physical problem does not make anatomical sense, and so it causes a problem for the doctor.[25] The conversion of mental suffering into a bodily symptom represents the unconscious mind communicating through body language. Once again, this is done in an unintentional, automatic manner. The hysteric does not know why she cannot use her leg, but she knows that she is suffering for an inexplicable reason. Through a process of unconscious association, the mind is able to utilize the body as a sign system in order to communicate through passive resistance.[26] In contemporary society, this hysterical use of the body is often evident in eating disorders and psychosomatic symptoms.

Traumatic Memory

From a postmodern perspective, our knowledge and values are always relative to our culture and time period, and so historical understanding is necessary to comprehend the content of cultural productions. For psychoanalysis, history is represented as memory, and memory is itself constantly being reconstructed from the perspective of the present. Freud therefore believes that sexuality represents a key to the unconscious because the initial infantile sexual experiences occur prior to the formation of sexual knowledge during puberty.[27] What then makes sexuality traumatic for the hysteric is that the memories of the early sexual experiences are re-interpreted from the perspective of later knowledge, and latency serves to separate the infantile from puberty by interjecting a sexual hiatus, which serves to repress infantile sexuality and produce a break between the sexual cause and the sexual effect.[28]

The hysterical subject is then traumatized by memories, but these memories are the result of a retroactive re-interpretation of meaning. In fact, we all have a hysterical core to our subjectivity because we do not retain any permanent memories from our first years of life.[29] In other words, our infancy is a black hole that can only be understood through the retroactive application of knowledge coming from others. Here we see how our unconscious emotions must be the result of the stories others tell us about our own past. Our origins are thus the effect of a retroactive reconstruction centered on the discourse of others. We literally only know about the content of our own emotions by imitating the responses of other people.

We shall see in the next chapter how Zizek absorbs this retroactive logic into the Hegelian dialectic, but for now, I want to focus on how pathos represents an unconscious mode of cultural and personal interpretation. One way of thinking about the psychoanalytic approach to the rhetoric of emotion is to look at how moods shape the ways people perceive the world.[30] For example, if a father comes home from a stressful day of work, and he becomes immediately angry at the sight of his messy house, we can see that he has been taken over by an emotion that dictates how he perceives the world around him. In a paranoid mode of thinking, he sees every physical sign of disorder as part of an entire interpretation of his social environment and condition. He thus experiences the world through the frame of his mood, and this mood is similar to a political ideology because it provides an instant, unconscious, and comprehensive interpretation. Every experience is connected to a sense of being exploited, abused, or victimized. His anger then is the result of magical thinking because he acts as if his criticism of his messy home can correct what happened outside of the house.[31] He has therefore displaced his anger onto a substituted context, but he is not aware of this substitution and displacement.

In terms of social movements, one of the issues is that people sometimes join groups in order to displace their emotions from their private lives.[32] Furthermore, group ideologies act as moods as they provide a comprehensive mode of interpretation from the perspective of a fantasy frame. For instance, the desire to blame all of the problems of the world on capitalism represents a totalizing perspective that blinds people from seeing some of the positive aspects of capitalism and the negative influences of other social and psychological factors. For Zizek, global capitalism often takes on the role of the traumatizing Other within the hysterical fantasy who is retroactively blamed for all of the problems of the world.

Zizek and the Global Monster of Capitalism

Before I get to how Zizek posits global capitalism as the ultimate traumatizing force in the world, it is important to stress that for Lacan, the fundamental conflict for human beings is the divide between the Symbolic and the Real. Since nothing lacks in the Real, and negativity can only be marked by the Symbolic, the fundamental trauma for all human beings is the imposition of language, which causes an alienation from the natural world.[33] It is the primary trauma that is re-interpreted and displaced by social and personal traumatic relations.

At times, Zizek does return to Lacan's notion that the Real is impossible to Symbolize, and therefore we are forever alienated from our inner and outer worlds:

> There is not just the interplay of appearances, there is a Real—this Real, however, is not the inaccessible Thing, but the gap which prevents our access to it, the "rock" of the antagonism which distorts our view of the perceived object through a partial perspective. The "truth" is thus not the

> "real" state of things, accessed by a "direct" view of the object without any perspectival distortion, but the very Real of the antagonism which causes the perspectival distortion itself. Again, the site of truth is not the way "things really are in themselves," beyond perspectival distortion, but the very gap or passage which separates one perspective from another, the gap (in this case, social antagonism) which makes the two perspectives radically incommensurable. The "Real as impossible" is the cause of the impossibility of our ever attaining the "neutral" non-perspectival view of the object. There is a truth, and not everything is relative—but this truth is the truth of the perspectival distortion as such, not a truth distorted by the partial view from a one-sided perspective. (*Less Than Nothing* 47–48)

The central idea here is that there is no neutral perspective one can take to examine the Real, since the impossibility of representing the Real means that all we can have is a partial, one-sided perspective. I believe that this argument represents a vital difference between Zizek and psychoanalysis because he is not just positing the unknowability of the thing-in-itself; rather, he is rationalizing the use of partisan, partial perspectives in contrast to the modern ideal of neutrality and impartiality.

As I will discuss in the fifth chapter of this book, modern democracy, sciences, and psychoanalysis are grounded on the necessary but impossible ideal of neutrality. Therefore, even if we have no direct access to the Real, we want our scientists and judges to make every effort to approach empirical evidence from an unbiased perspective. Here we see how a certain idealism does shape our everyday lives and allows for social institutions and practices to be built around the human construction of the ideal of neutrality. It is in fact the invention of this ideal that signals the fundamental shift from premodernity to modernity: if we can say that in the premodern world, the king is the law, but in the modern world, the law is the king, it is because modern democracy is derived from an investment in the ideal of the neutral judge divorced from any divine or natural order. This neutrality enables universality and equality because it establishes a separation from self-interest and social hierarchy. Of course, this universal equality and neutrality often fails, but we know that it has failed because we compare it to the ideal.

In the case of psychoanalysis, the neutrality of the analyst enables the patent to try to take a neutral perspective in relation to desires, thoughts, and feelings. Thus by suspending judgment and by not mirroring the ideas of the patient or fulfilling the demands of the patient, the analyst produces an artificial relationship that enables an encounter with the truth of the patient's reality. However, as Freud stresses, science is predicated on realizing that we can never know the whole truth, and what determines the movement from primitive animism to religion and finally to science is the acceptance of the limits of our own thinking.[34]

Freud posited that in the first stages of life and civilization, there is no clear distinction between thoughts and perceptions, and so our primary mode of thinking is hallucination.[35] In what he called the "omnipotence of thought," Freud described "primitive" cultures as determined by an animistic worldview where inner thoughts were confused with external perceptions, and it is only with science, that humans are able to use the reality principle to fully differentiate between our thoughts and the external world.

According to this theory of the primary processes in the unconscious, what allows us to see the world from a partisan perspective is our failure to separate our thoughts from our perceptions, and from this perspective, subjective feelings and political ideologies work against the reality principle and the possibilities of science and democracy. Here we see how personal and political emotions are derived from unconscious processes centered on equating inner thoughts with the outer world. In the case of political polarization, each side views the world from a distorted perspective because each side rejects the possibility of a neutral, non-partisan perspective.[36] In fact, Zizek turns to Marx to argue that we can only read the past and the present through the lens of conflict and partisanship: "Marx claims that the bourgeoisie is the first class in the history of humanity which is posited as such, as a class, so that it is only with the rise of capitalism that the entirety of history hitherto becomes readable as the history of class struggle" (*Less Than Nothing* 7). The argument here is that class struggle is the lens that gives us access to the truth of history, since we can only read reality from a partisan view. From this perspective, neutrality is impossible, and so there can only be division and pathos.

It has been my argument here that the rhetoric of emotion helps to explain the fundamental hysteria of social movements that rely on taking a divisive and partisan perspective. While it is necessary to use pathos to motivate and consolidate a collective group, this partisan perspective eventually runs into conflict with the desire for fair and equal treatment. Since modern law has to be neutral, equal, and universal, it has to suspend partisan perspectives as it attempts to apply reason from a neutral judgment. However, in order for this universal law to be expanded so that it includes previously excluded groups, it is necessary for a dialectical relation to be established between postmodern minority-based social movements and modern universality. In other words, the universal is dynamic, and there is an inner tension between equality and identity politics, but this tension is necessary and productive.

Since Zizek tends to privilege a Marxist vision of class conflict over identity politics and modern neutrality, his partisan perspective does not allow for the necessary relation between postmodern social movements and modern equality. Moreover, by displacing the conflict between the Symbolic and the Real onto the conflict between neutrality and partisanship, his work functions to naturalize an antagonistic perspective, and like all antagonisms, this conflict produces drama and affect, but it does not allow a space for modern science, democracy, and psychoanalysis.

This use of pathos by Zizek is often centered on his post-Marxist argument that in our contemporary globalized economy, capitalism is an amorphous monster threatening all aspects of our lives:

> [H]e [Marx] could not yet imagine the way abstraction rules would develop in capitalism: when Marx describes capital's mad self-enhancing circulation, which reaches its apogee in today's meta-reflexive speculations on futures, it is far too simplistic to claim that the specter of this self-engendering monster pursuing its interests with no regard for human or environmental concerns is an ideological abstraction, and that, behind this abstraction, there are real people and natural objects on whose productive capacities and resources capital's circulation is based and on which it feeds like a gigantic parasite. The problem is that this "abstraction" is not only characteristic of our (the financial speculator's) misperception of social reality, but that it is "real" in the precise sense of determining the structure of material social processes themselves: the fate of whole swathes of the population and sometimes of whole countries can be decided by the "solipsistic" speculative dance of Capital, which pursues its goal of profitability with blessed indifference to how its movements will affect social reality. Therein lies the fundamental systemic violence of capitalism, much more uncanny than the direct pre-capitalist socio-ideological violence: it is no longer attributable to concrete individuals and their "evil" intentions, but is purely "objective," systemic, anonymous. (*Less Than Nothing* 244)

The pathos generated by this extreme rhetoric is in part due to the universalizing claims concerning a violent order that is systemic and anonymous. Moreover, Zizek collapses the difference between the Symbolic and the

Real by positing that the capitalist Symbolic system of exchange value has replaced reality with pure abstraction.

Instead of representing the Real as that which is impossible to Symbolize, Zizek insists that global capitalism is the Real itself:

> Here we encounter the Lacanian difference between reality and the Real: "reality" is the social reality of the actual people involved in interaction and in the productive processes, while the Real is the inexorable "abstract" spectral logic of Capital that determines what goes on in social reality. This gap is tangible in the way the economic situation of a country can be considered to be good and stable by the international financial experts, even when the majority of its people are worse off than before—reality does not matter, what matters is the situation of Capital. And, again, is this not more true than ever today? Do not phenomena usually classed as features of "virtual capitalism" (future trading and similar financial speculations) point towards the reign of "real abstraction" at its purest, much more radical than in Marx's time? In short, the highest form of ideology does not involve getting caught in ideological spectrality, forgetting about real people and their relations, but precisely in overlooking this Real of spectrality and in pretending to address directly "real people with their real problems." Visitors to the London Stock Exchange are given a free leaflet explaining how the stock market is not about mysterious fluctuations, but about real people and their products—this is ideology at its purest. (244–245)

Driven by his desire to represent global capitalism as the ultimate evil, Zizek dismisses the importance of considering real people with real problems because what matters is the abstract understanding of capitalist abstraction. My goal here is not to dismiss the destructive effects of global capitalism; instead, I believe it is important to understand how a certain Leftist rhetoric is dedicated to scaring people into a state of alarm but also helplessness. After all, why resist or fight anything if we can do nothing against an all-encompassing force of anonymous Symbolic violence. For example, in the fight against climate change, it is necessary to affirm a distance between "Symbolic" global capitalism and the "Real" natural world because if we do not make this distinction, then we have nothing to fight against.

However, instead of insisting on the difference between Symbolic abstraction and the resistances of the Real, Zizek turns to Hegel to reverse Marx's reversal of German Idealism:

> Here, in the analysis of the universe of Capital, we should not only push Hegel towards Marx, Marx himself should be radicalized: it is only today, in relation to global capitalism in its "post-industrial" form, that, to put it in Hegelian terms, really existing capitalism is reaching the level of its notion. Perhaps, we should once again follow Marx's old anti-evolutionist motto (incidentally, taken verbatim from Hegel) that the anatomy of man provides the key to the anatomy of a monkey—i.e., that, in order to describe the inherent notional structure of a social formation, we must start with its most developed form. Marx located the elementary capitalist antagonism in the opposition between use-value and exchange-value: in capitalism, the potential of this opposition is fully realized, the domain of exchange-value acquires autonomy, is transformed into the specter of self-propelling speculative capital which uses the productive capacities and needs of actual people only as its temporary disposable embodiment. Marx derived his notion of economic crisis from this very gap: a crisis occurs when reality catches up with the illusory self- generating mirage of money begetting more money—this speculative madness cannot go on indefinitely, it has to explode in ever more serious crises. The ultimate root of the crisis is for Marx the gap between use- and exchange-value: the logic of exchange-value follows its own path, its own mad dance, irrespective of the real needs of real people. (245)

By removing real people from the mad dance of capitalism, Zizek eliminates the possibility of freedom, responsibility, and change; in this extreme rhetoric of pathos, there is no space for logos or ethos, since people are simply the disposable parts of an all-consuming global force.

From Zizek's pathos-laden perspective, as an irrational social system spreads to all parts of the world and all aspects of life, the only cause for every social problem is pure Hegelian abstraction derived from the capitalist virtualization of reality:

> It may appear that this analysis is highly relevant today, when the tension between the virtual universe and the real is reaching almost unbearable proportions: on the one hand, we have crazy solipsistic speculations about futures, mergers, etc., following their own inherent logic; on the other hand, reality is catching up in the guise of ecological catastrophes, poverty, the collapse of social life in the Third World, and the spread of new diseases. (245)

This all-encompassing worldview eliminates all differences and provides an extremist partisan perspective disabling any other theories or explanations. Global capitalism is here imagined to be the ultimate victimizing force subjecting all aspects of human life to an irrational mode of Symbolic violence.

Since global capitalism is presented as a virtual force of Symbolic abstraction replacing the Real with a system of irrational violence and exchange, there can be no space left for a neutral perspective or a mediating social intervention:

> This is why cyber-capitalists appear as the paradigmatic capitalists today—why Bill Gates can dream of cyberspace as providing the frame for what he calls "frictionless capitalism." What we have here is an ideological short- circuit between two versions of the gap between reality and virtuality: the gap between real production and the virtual or spectral domain of Capital, and the gap between experiential reality and the virtual reality of cyberspace. The real horror of the motto "frictionless capitalism" is that, even though actual "frictions" continue to insist, they become invisible, forced into a netherworld outside our "postmodern" and post-industrial universe; this is why the "frictionless" universe of digitalized communication, technological gadgets, etc., is constantly haunted by the notion of a global catastrophe lurking just around the corner, threatening to explode at any moment. (245–246)

This depiction of the "horrors" of virtual global capitalism takes on the pathos of a horror film where an unstoppable monster threatens our very existence. Of course, the Left has often used the threat of a catastrophe to scare people into fighting back against injustice and violence, but with Zizek's rhetoric, it is unclear what one is fighting or how we can fight back.

As we shall see in the next chapter, the way that Zizek seeks to overcome the fundamental conflicts he examines is through his return to Hegel. I will argue that what he gets from this thinker is a way of reconciling opposites through the manipulation of self-reflexive language. This overcoming of social differences presents ethos as the appeal to a higher authority in a relationship of narcissistic transference. In other words, by becoming the one who understands his idealized Other, he is able to idealize his own work as he uses meta-language and metacognition to close the gap between the Symbolic and the Real.

Notes

1. Halliwell, Stephen. *Aristotle's poetics*. University of Chicago Press, 1998.
2. Scheff, Thomas J. *Catharsis in healing, ritual, and drama*. University of California Press, 1979.

3. Freud, Sigmund. "Project for a scientific psychology (1950 [1895])." *The Standard Edition of the Complete Psychological Works of Sigmund Freud, Volume I (1886–1899): Pre-Psycho-Analytic Publications and Unpublished Drafts.* 1966. 281–391.
4. Freud, Sigmund. "Remembering, repeating and working-through (Further recommendations on the technique of psycho-analysis II)." *The Standard Edition of the Complete Psychological Works of Sigmund Freud, Volume XII (1911–1913): The Case of Schreber, Papers on Technique and Other Works.* 1958. 145–156.
5. See Chapter Two of Samuels, Robert. *Freud for the Twenty-First Century: The Science of Everyday Life.* Springer, 2019.
6. Hilgard, Ernest R. "Impulsive versus realistic thinking: An examination of the distinction between primary and secondary processes in thought." *Psychological Bulletin* 59.6 (1962): 477.
7. Freud, Sigmund. *Group psychology and the analysis of the ego.* WW Norton & Company, 1975.
8. Samuels, Robert. "Victim Politics: Psychoanalyzing the Neoliberal Conservative Counter-Revolution." *Psychoanalyzing the Left and Right after Donald Trump.* Palgrave Macmillan, Cham, 2016. 7–29.
9. Christie, Nils. "The ideal victim." *From crime policy to victim policy.* Palgrave Macmillan, London, 1986. 17–30.
10. Berrey, Ellen. *The enigma of diversity: The language of race and the limits of racial justice.* University of Chicago Press, 2015.
11. De Cock, Christian, and Steffen Böhm. "Liberalist fantasies: Žižek and the impossibility of the open society." *Organization* 14.6 (2007): 815–836.
12. Marx, Karl, and Friedrich Engels. *The communist manifesto.* Penguin, 2002.
13. Butler, Judith, et al. *Contingency, hegemony, universality: Contemporary dialogues on the left.* Verso, 2000.
14. Yarom, Nitza. "A matrix of hysteria." *International Journal of Psycho-Analysis* 78 (1997): 1119–1134.
15. Nishida, Tracy K., and Angeline S. Lillard. "The informative value of emotional expressions: 'Social referencing' in mother–child pretense." *Developmental Science* 10.2 (2007): 205–212.
16. Von Scheve, Christian. "Collective emotions." *The Wiley-Blackwell Encyclopedia of Social Theory* (2017): 1–3.
17. Dean, Jodi. *Solidarity of strangers: Feminism after identity politics.* University of California Press, 1996.
18. Bondi, Liz. "Locating identity politics." *Place and the Politics of Identity.* Routledge, 2004. 89–106.
19. Faller, Kathleen Coulborn. "Is the child victim of sexual abuse telling the truth?." *Child Abuse & Neglect* 8.4 (1984): 473–481.

20. Hook, Derek. "Lacan, the meaning of the phallus and the 'sexed' subject." (2006): 60–84.
21. Stevenson, Dina. "Lacan, Burke, and the human motive." *Kenneth Burke and the twenty-first century* (1999): 191–206.
22. Showalter, Elaine. *Hystories: Hysterical epidemics and modern media*. Vol. 2. Columbia University Press, 1997.
23. Smith, Bruce R. "Premodern sexualities." *Publications of The Modern Language Association Of America* (2000): 318–329.
24. Dane, Gabrielle. "Hysteria as Feminist Protest: Dora, Cixous, Acker." *Women's Studies: An Interdisciplinary Journal* 23.3 (1994): 231–255.
25. McGrath, William. *Freud's discovery of psychoanalysis: The politics of hysteria*. Ithaca: Cornell University Press, 1986.
26. Kristeva, Julia. *Revolution in poetic language*. Columbia University Press, 1984.
27. Bistoen, Gregory, Stijn Vanheule, and Stef Craps. "Nachträglichkeit: A Freudian perspective on delayed traumatic reactions." *Theory & Psychology* 24.5 (2014): 668–687.
28. Freud, Sigmund. "Three essays on the theory of sexuality (1905)." *The Standard Edition of the Complete Psychological Works of Sigmund Freud, Volume VII (1901–1905): A Case of Hysteria, Three Essays on Sexuality and Other Works*. 1953. 123–246.
29. Dudycha, George J., and Martha M. Dudycha. "Childhood memories: a review of the literature." *Psychological Bulletin* 38.8 (1941): 668.
30. Furukawa, Toshi A. "Assessment of mood: guides for clinicians." *Journal of Psychosomatic Research* 68.6 (2010): 581–589.
31. Sartre, Jean-Paul. *Sketch for a Theory of the Emotions*. Routledge, 2015.
32. Kaplan, Howard B., and Xiaoru Liu. "Social movements as collective coping with spoiled personal identities: Intimations from a panel study of changes in the life course between adolescence and adulthood." *Self, identity, and social movements* (2000): 215–238.
33. Lacan, Jacques. "The subversion of the subject and the dialectic of desire in the Freudian unconscious." *Hegel and Contemporary Continental Philosophy* 19.6 (1960): 205–235.
34. Samuels, Robert. "Science and the Reality Principle." *Freud for the Twenty-First Century*. Palgrave Pivot, Cham, 2019. 5–16.
35. Freud, Sigmund. *Totem and Taboo: Some Points of Agreement between the Mental Lives of Savages and Neurotics*. Routledge, 2013.
36. Prior, Markus. "Media and political polarization." *Annual Review of Political Science* 16 (2013): 101–127.

CHAPTER 4

Ethos, Transference, and Liberal Cynicism

Abstract This chapter examines the rhetorical form of ethos in Zizek's work as it relates to the psychoanalytic concepts of transference and narcissism. In Zizek's work, Hegel is idealized in the transference as the one who already knows. As a form of cynical conformity, Zizek relies on an atheistic use of Christianity in order to posit an ideal Other who verifies his ideal ego in a narcissistic structure. For Aristotle, ethos represents the character of the speaker in a defined social hierarchy.

Keywords Zizek • Hegel • Aristotle • Narcissism • Transference • Cynical conformity

One of the main questions of psychoanalysis is the issue of why do people freely choose to submit to a higher power?[1] For Freud, he first encountered this issue when he started to hypnotize his patients and realized that they would do and think whatever he suggested.[2] Even after Freud gave up this oppressive method, he continued to notice the ways patients would seek to submit to his will. He would later call this type of relationship "transference," but it is important to look at his initial understanding of this structure in order to see how ideology functions in the world today.[3]

In his *Project for a Scientific Psychology*, Freud posited that when an infant encounters an unmet need, the first response is to hallucinate the satisfaction of the wish. Here we find the dominance of the primary

R. Samuels, *Zizek and the Rhetorical Unconscious*,
https://doi.org/10.1007/978-3-030-50910-1_4

process in the unconscious, which serves to realize the cathartic goal of the pleasure principle. However, when this act of hallucination or imagination does not resolve the problem, the child will cry in order to get someone else to make the suffering go away. This relationship defines transference as the transferring of responsibility for achieving the pleasure principle from the subject to the Other. Instead of imagining the satisfaction of desire, one makes a demand to another person to have the desire fulfilled. Moreover, our dependence on other people stems in part from the fact that humans are born premature, because unlike other animals, it takes us a long time to stand up and fend for ourselves.[4] Our dependency on others is thus derived from our extended helplessness.

For Freud, this cry to the Other represents the foundation of both communication and morality. Since the child is making a demand to the Other, it is necessary for this other person to understand what the cry means; the social use of language can therefore be understood as generated from a primal demand for help. Furthermore, this structure is defined by an unequal relation between the helpless subject and the powerful Other.[5] From an evolutionary perspective, we can see that due to the extended helplessness of the human infant, survival requires communication.

Lacan argues that when a child makes a demand to the parent for the satisfaction of a desire, the demand is not just for the particular object, but for recognition, love, and understanding.[6] After all, the helping Other has to understand what the demand means and has to first recognize the value of responding to the demand in an act of care and love. Lacan added that in analysis, the patient comes into treatment with a demand for help and assumes that the analyst is the one who knows how to help.[7] Thus, in the relationship of transference, the analyst is placed in the position of the powerful, helping parent who is expected to know, love, and recognize the patient's desire.

According to Freud, this primary relationship between the helpless child and the all-powerful parent influences all social and personal relationships. For example, he interprets religious prayer as a demand made to a powerful Other to change reality and satisfy the pleasure principle.[8] Psychoanalysis then is a process of trying to move away from transference by creating a situation where the Other does not respond to the demands of the subject. From this perspective, psychoanalysis is a social practice that seeks to use, expose, and then eliminate transference.

Ethos and Transference

In terms of rhetoric, ethos utilizes transference, since it is based on the recognized authority of the speaker, and as Aristotle posits, this authority or character is determined by the position of the authority in a particular social hierarchy.[9] Within the term "authority," we find the word author, and this indicates how ethos is founded on the unequal relationship between someone with power and an audience that submits to that power. In other words, ethos is a form of transference that re-enacts the fundamental relationship between the helpless infant and the all-powerful parent. Moreover, the authority of ethos is derived from the Other occupying the position of the one who is supposed to know.[10]

In opposition to premodern ethos, modern logos or reason is supposed to replace the reliance on external authority with the scientific testing of reality and the institution of democratic equality.[11] Within a premodern society, the king or the priest or the father is the ultimate source of ethos and authority, but in modernity, the law is ideally universal and neutral. Furthermore, the liberation of the subject from premodern authority and belief creates a space for modern individuality and the protection of individual rights based on individual responsibility. Modernity is then itself structured by an internal conflict between the impersonal law and the liberated individual.

As we saw in the analysis of postmodern hysteria and social movements on the Left, pathos is often generated from the conflicts between premodern hierarchy and modern equality. In contrast, one of the goals of post-postmodern ideology is to resolve this conflict on an Imaginary level by combining together premodern ethos with modern liberation: the central ideological trick is how to get people to freely choose their submission to social authority as the conflict between pre-modernity and modernity is overcome.[12]Furthermore, a fundamental problem in contemporary society is how to establish ethos (authority) in a cultural that has called into question all past, premodern authorities.

In the case of Zizek's work, the central way that he takes on the position of the one who knows is through his idealization of the work of Hegel, and the reason why Hegel is such a good source of ethos for Zizek is because this German Idealist developed an ideology that solves the conflict between premodernity and modernity. As I will show in my reading of Hegel's ideology and Zizek's use of this ideology, one of philosophy's central task can be considered to be the anticipation of the ideal reconciliation of social conflict.

Hegel's Ethos and Ideology

The first way that Hegel resolves the divide between the premodern and the modern is by his use of the term "Geist."[13] In his *Phenomenology of the Mind* (Geist), this term can indicate both mind and spirit, and through the double meaning of this signifier, he is able to combine together premodern religion (spirit) and modern science (mind). The conflict between premodern authority and modern reason is therefore overcome on a purely linguistic level, which points to Freud's idea that words at first all had opposite meanings, and on the level of the unconscious, symbols can represent two conflicting ideas at the same time.[14]

Another basic way that Hegel uses language to overcome conflict is by arguing that when someone says "I," they are making a personal reference, but since anyone can say "I," this term is both the most universal and the most particular signifier, and therefore, there is no difference between the universal and the particular. Individuality then no longer conflicts with the impersonal universal law of science and democracy, since the individual is seen as being universal, and the universal is considered to be individual.

It is then the use of language that in part allows for Hegel's idealism and ideology, and we can consider much of his work as an attempt to use language to understand language and to create a meta-language where the problems of thought are resolved through the production of a self-reflexive discourse. This thinking about thinking in philosophy often results in an obsessional discourse where one attempts to mediate real conflicts by resolving the divide between the Symbolic and the Real on the level of the Imaginary. To understand this structure, however, we have to first comprehend how transference relates to narcissism.

Transference and Narcissism

Lacan argues that in the structure of narcissism, the subject seeks to have the ideal ego recognized by the ego ideal.[15] In other words, one desires to have the good version of the self verified by an uncritical Other, and Lacan uses his theory of the mirror stage to explain how both the ideal self and the ideal Other are produced. In the paradigmatic scene of ego formation, a subject looks into the mirror and sees itself as an ideal, unified image with a clear boundary between the internal and the external world.[16] This distinction between the inside and the outside is made possible through the identification with the body as a container with a defined border. Since we never see our body in its entirety, our relation to our body is considered to be Imaginary and virtual; the gaps in our vision are filled in by the identification with a coherent whole in the form of a Gestalt image. The ego therefore comes into being through an identification with an external image or by identifying with someone of a similar size and shape.

Lacan adds that when the child looks into the mirror and sees its own reflection, it gains a sense of its self as separate and coherent. This occurs at a time when the child is just learning how to stand up and control his or her own body. The sense of self-unity and bodily control is thus derived from the identification with the other in a primary relation of alienation and the anticipation of ideal self-control. Lacan adds that often the child will first look at the image in the mirror and then will look back at a parent behind the child in order to see the Other recognizing the ideal image.[17] This is the structure of secondary narcissism because one demands that the Other recognize the ideal self. In contemporary culture, this structure is evident in the social media site Facebook, where people posit images of themselves to an audience who is then asked to "like" the representation. Here, the Other plays the role of the authority (ethos) who is asked to recognize the satisfaction (catharsis) of the externalized ego.

Freud examined this connection between narcissism and transference in the Rat Man case where he discovered that this obsessional subject would not reveal the truth about his own desires because he wanted Freud to see him as a good person.[18] Obsessional narcissism then represents a double alienation because one is dependent on the Other to recognize an idealized sense of the self, which is itself derived from an identification with an ideal external image or other. This narcissistic transference helps to explain why some liberals are obsessed by having their good intentions and acts recognized by other people: since they want to repress their sense of shame and guilt, they have to engage in external rituals of purification.[19] For an obsessional compulsive neurotic, this desire for purification may result in obsessive hand washing, but for contemporary liberals, purification can be demonstrated by recycling, eating organic food, driving hybrid cars, or having a friend who is a person of color.[20] While there is nothing wrong with these acts in themselves, the problem is that they often represent an attempt of a person to have their good self recognized by others, and this desire for purity causes the repression of impure thoughts and feelings into the unconscious.

As Freud discovered, the desire to be seen as good and pure often results in the denial of aggressive feelings and actions and the projection of this aggression onto others. Freud went as far as saying that behind every good intention, there is an evil desire.[21] For Lacan, this aggression is in part derived from the fact that if the good self is reliant on identifying with the image of the good other, then one will feel an unconscious sense of resentment toward the satisfied other.[22] Moreover, this need to have the good self recognized by the ideal Other results in a repression of the super-ego into the unconscious as an attempt to repress any feelings of guilt or shame.

One of the goals of analysis is to suspend this narcissistic structure of transference through the neutrality of the analyst and the free association of the patient.[23] Since the patient is supposed to speak without thinking about the judgments of the analyst, the narcissistic transference is suspended. Unfortunately, few people inside or outside of psychoanalysis understand this process, and so they tend to believe that they key to analysis is the use of empathy and understanding.[24] In most forms of therapy, the therapist believes that one has to understand the patient and feel what the patient is feeling, but Lacan argued that these good intentions make neutrality and free association impossible.[25] While I will discuss this issue in the next chapter, what I want to turn to now is how Zizek engages in a narcissistic transference with Hegel.

Saving Hegel

A recurrent move in much academic discourse is to discover someone from the past who already anticipated the problems of the present.[26] In a process of transference and ethos, one identifies with the idealized authority who knows, and through this identification, one also becomes someone who knows. For Zizek, it is Hegel who already knows, and so he tries to purify Hegel's thought and remove him from accusation of being a totalitarian thinker who resolves every problem on an Imaginary level.

Throughout his book *Less Than Nothing*, Zizek seeks to defend Hegel against criticism:[27]

> According to this critique, the Hegelian reconciliation is false because it occurs only in the Idea, while real antagonisms persist—in the "concrete"

> experience of the "real life" of individuals who cling to their particular identity, state power remains an external compulsion. Therein resides the crux of the young Marx's critique of Hegel's political thought: Hegel presents the modern constitutional monarchy as a rational State in which antagonisms are reconciled, as an organic Whole in which every constituent finds, or can find, its proper place, but he thereby obfuscates the class antagonism which continues in modern societies, generating the working class as the "non-reason of the existing Reason," as the part of modern society which has no proper part in it, as its "part of no-part" (Rancière). (201)

In this passage, Zizek reiterates one of the fundamental criticisms of Hegel's work, which is that he presents an ideal reconciliation of social conflicts through the Imaginary integration of premodern organic life and the modern rational state.

According to Zizek, one way that this overcoming of conflict is achieved in Hegel is through a retroactive vision based on the equivalence of opposites:

> This is how Hegelian reconciliation works—not as a positive gesture of resolving or overcoming the conflict, but as a retroactive insight into how there never really was a serious conflict, how the two opponents were always on the same side. (204)

The conflicts between religion and science, the self and the other, language and the Real, and nature and culture are therefore transcended by an ideal view combining opposites together. Just as in the mirror stage, the self comes into being by identifying with the other and seeing its ideal self verified by an imagined ideal Other, we can understand the Imaginary role of ideology as a double form of alienation: one not only sees the world from the perspective of the Other, but sees one's own self through an identification with an ideal image of unity, coherency, and totality.[28] Within this structure, ethos is determined by the subject taking on the view of the Other as if that perspective is coming from the self.

As we learn from Zizek, the relation to the Ethos of the ideal Other is always retroactive, since the subject must see the past from the perspective of the present:

> The dialectical process is thus more refined than it may appear: the standard notion is that one can only arrive at the final truth along the path of error, so that the errors along the way are not simply discarded, but "sublated" in

> the final truth, preserved in it as its moments. The evolutionary notion of dialectical process tells us that the result is not just a dead body, that it does not stand alone, in abstraction from the process that engendered it: in this process, different moments first appeared in their unilateral immediate form, while the final synthesis gathers them as sublated, maintaining their rational core. What this standard notion misses is how the previous moments are preserved precisely as superfluous. In other words, while the preceding stages are indeed superfluous, we need time to arrive at the point from which we can see that they are so. (206–207)

I believe that what Zizek and Hegel are describing as a universal process of retroactive understanding is actually an obsessional discourse centered on the desire to know and see everything through the agency of an already established Symbolic knowledge: thus, the reason why the obsessional may not be able to sleep at night is that he cannot stop trying to resolve the conflict between Symbolic knowledge and reality.[29] Instead of accepting the fundamental divide between the Symbolic and the Real, obsessional subjects try to reconcile this difference on the level of pure thought. However, since this reconciliation is ultimately impossible, one can only constantly repeat the same failed attempt at overcoming this divide. In Zizek's case, this type of obsessional repetition is manifested in his continual reiteration of the same arguments and examples.[30] He cannot stop recycling his own work because all he can do is repeat that same misencounter with the Real.

Hegel then is the perfect author for Zizek to repeat because Hegel himself constantly repeats the same formal logic of the dialectical attempt to overcome all differences. In this structure, the Symbolic knowledge is already there, and what the subject has to do is find its place in the perspective of the Other:

> "Freedom" is thus inherently retroactive: at its most elementary, it is not simply a free act which, out of nowhere, starts a new causal link, but a retroactive act of determining which link or sequence of necessities will determine us. (213)

This definition of human freedom is structured by the notion that our present world is already predetermined, and so the only thing we can do is to change our perspective of the past. If this theory appears to harken back to the Christian notion of predetermination, it is because Hegel and Zizek are at times combining together premodern religion with modern individualism:

> In predestination, fate is substantialized into a decision that precedes the process, so that the burden of individuals' activities is not to performatively constitute their fate, but to discover (or guess) their pre-existing fate. What is thereby obfuscated is the dialectical reversal of contingency into necessity, that is, the way the outcome of a contingent process takes on the appearance of necessity: things retroactively "will have been" necessary. (213)

From a premodern perspective, the fate of the individual is predetermined by god who has authorized the social hierarchy, but from a modern perspective, people are free to use their reason to determine their own fate; the way, then, to overcome this opposition is to posit that people are free to interpret their contingent lives as being necessary from a retroactive perspective. In fact, from the position of the present, everything that happened to us in the past is necessary because it all contributes to the present moment: if one thing didn't happen in the past, our present would be different. This type of thinking represents a key insight into obsessional thinking: in an effort to make Symbolic knowledge match the Real, contingent knowledge must be seen as necessary.

Christianity and Cynical Conformity

A fundamental issue of contemporary society is how to reconcile premodern religion with modern atheistic science. While Hegel uses language to make these opposite worlds coincide, Zizek's central rhetorical strategy is a form of cynical conformity.[31] As a dominant mode of subjectivity in contemporary life, cynical conformity means that people conform to a system in which they do not believe. In Zizek's case, his constant references to Christianity can be read as cynical, since he declares that he is an atheist. From a historical perspective, we see that he is able to both affirm and reject religion through a contradictory and ironic use of language. For example, in the following passage, Christianity represents the ethos of the ideal Other, since what the obsessional seeks is a dead Imaginary father who can only recognize the subject's good self:[32]

> This, perhaps, would have been the ultimate meaning of the singularity of Christ's incarnation: it is an act which radically changes our destiny. Prior to

> Christ, we were determined by Fate, caught up in the cycle of sin and its payment; but Christ's erasure of our past sins means precisely that his sacrifice changes our virtual past and thus sets us free. (213)

While it is clear that Zizek does not actually believe in Christ's reincarnation, he uses the dead figure of Christ to add ethos to his argument. From an obsessional perspective, everything in life can be explained by an unconscious belief in predestination: the obsessional is superstitious because as Freud posited, the modern subject has internalized premodern religion on an individual, unconscious basis.[33] The obsessional thinks that everything happens for a reason, and he is fated to suffer, but he also thinks that he is free and can escape his fate.

The contradictory nature of Zizek's discourse is in part derived from his simultaneous belief that we cannot escape our historically defined knowledge and his desire for a universal perspective. This ideological contradiction is present in his reading of Marx:

> Marx himself nonetheless comes close to this paradox of non-teleological retroactivity when, in his Grundrisse manuscripts, apropos the notion of labor, he pointed out how even the most abstract categories, despite their validity—precisely because of their abstractness—for all epochs, are nevertheless, in the specific character of this abstraction, themselves likewise a product of historic relations, and possess their full validity only for and within these relations. Bourgeois society is the most developed and the most complex historic organization of production. The categories which express its relations, the comprehension of its structure, thereby also allows insights into the structure and the relations of production of all the vanished social formations out of whose ruins and elements it built itself up, whose partly still unconquered remnants are carried along within it, whose mere nuances have developed explicit significance within it, etc. Human anatomy contains a key to the anatomy of the ape. The intimations of higher development among the subordinate animal species, however, can be understood only after the higher development is already known. In short, to paraphrase Pierre Bayard, what Marx is saying here is that the anatomy of the ape, although it was formed earlier in time than the anatomy of man, nonetheless in a certain way plagiarizes by anticipation the anatomy of man. (220–221)

This retroactive evolutionary theory explains the foundation of obsessional ethos in the age of cynical conformity: we are trapped by social systems and historical understandings in which we no longer believe but which we treat as being necessary.[34] From a postmodern perspective of pathos, the conflict between premodern social determinism and modern freedom results in anxiety and tension, but from a post-postmodern perspective, anxiety and conflict are repressed by combining conformity with disbelief. There can be no conflict if one does not believe in the knowledge one is repeating.

Zizek then presents a discourse that combines together two belief systems (Christianity and Marxism) in which he no longer believes:

> As Hegel already showed apropos the dialectic of Enlightenment and faith in his Phenomenology of Spirit, such an opposition of formal Enlightenment and fundamental-substantial beliefs is false, an untenable ideologico-existential position. What should be done is to fully assume the identity of the two opposed moments, which is precisely what apocalyptic "Christian materialism" can do: it brings together the rejection of divine Otherness and the unconditional commitment. (224)

This return to discredited religion and politics represents a fundamental problem of contemporary ethos; how does one appeal to authority when all social hierarchies have been called into question?[35]

As we have seen, in our post-authority culture, the narcissistic transference uses ethos in a cynical fashion. Like a zombie that is dead but continues to haunt our existence, old ideas from religion and politics repeat in our discourses. Philosophy, then, seeks to re-animate these past traditions in a retroactive fashion where we are predetermined by a culture in which we no longer believe. Through a culture of re-mixing and recycling, we cannot escape these discredited ideologies, and so all Zizek can do is to repeat the missed encounter with modernity.

Zizek's theory of cynical conformity can be explained in his story about the Neils Bohr. Supposedly, someone who was visiting the physicist saw a horseshoe above his door. When they asked him if he believed in the superstition that it brings good luck, he replied that of course he doesn't, but he was told it works even if you don't believe in it. Zizek's analysis of this story is the following: "This is indeed how ideology functions today: nobody takes democracy or justice seriously, we are all aware of their corrupted nature, but we participate in them, we display our belief in them, because we assume that they work even if we do not believe in them."[36] Cynical conformity is therefore the perfect ideology for post-belief liberalism; people conform to the system because it is the only game in town, and what matters is not what they think, but what they think other people think. Due to the loss of belief in premodern authority, ethos can only be generated through this mode of cynical conformity.

Obama and Liberal Cynicism

In terms of contemporary politics and culture, cynical conformity helps us to explain the liberal investment in meritocracy and education as the solution to all social problems.[37] Since schools are centered now on ranking, grading, and rating everything, they provide a good source for the production of ego ideals to which the liberal subject attempts to conform. A meritocratic system, which is no longer based on the aristocratic premodern order of inherited social authority, relies on people freely agreeing to have their personal worth judged by established social norms.[38] Even if people know the system is no longer primarily about learning, or they see how it reinforces inequality, they still conform to the system out of fear of being beaten out by other conformists.[39]

President Obama was a great example of liberal narcissism because he not only thought that education was the solution to economic inequality, but also relied on a type of warfare that removes direct responsibility.[40] In his usage of drones as a central part of his military strategy, he employed a weapon that is void of direct human contact. As a form of "clean war," the drone allows one to fight as a distance without having to risk the lives of your own people.[41] The drone is therefore a perfect weapon for a liberal culture that does not want to feel guilty for its own aggression.

While many argue that Obama did not have a choice but to confirm to the current system, especially because his blackness made him vulnerable to racists attacks, it is clear that he surrounded himself with political insiders who came mostly from the elite liberal professional upper class.[42] Even his healthcare plan, which did help millions of people get health insurance, was designed with pharmaceutical companies and was first articulated by a conservative think tank.[43] Meanwhile his reactions to the financial crisis of 2008 consisted mostly of saving the banks and not the homeowners.[44] From this perspective, we can see Obama's liberalism as an attempt to sure up the status quo in order to keep the system going at all costs.

While Obama was the most cosmopolitan and globalist president ever, his election can be seen as a part of liberal tokenism.[45] Since liberals want to feel that they are good people, they want to assuage their guilt for a racist culture by promoting a select few people of color to positions of prominence.[46] However, as we saw during Obama's presidency, this strategy did not improve the lives of most African Americans citizens.[47] Instead, of developing programs that would help the poor, Obama centered his attention on conforming to the very system that continues to discriminate against people of color. As a symbol of ethos during a period where the belief in authority has been called into question, Obama can be read as a cultural ideal divorced from reality. Although much pathos and enthusiasm was generated by his election, this emotional investment in hope and change did not actually end up changing much. Instead, he helped to provide catharsis to a liberal professional class that recognizes inequality but does not know what to do about it.

The next chapter will attempt to provide an alternative to the rhetoric of catharsis, pathos, and ethos. By turning to Freud's method and his theory of logos in the form of the reality principle, I will provide a foundation for thinking about the roles of science, democracy, and capitalism in our globalizing world. Part of this analysis will require a critique of Zizek's rejection of neutrality and his projection of social conflicts into the real.

Notes

1. Fromm, Erich. *Escape from freedom*. Macmillan, 1994.
2. Freud, Sigmund. "Hypnosis." *The Standard Edition of the Complete Psychological Works of Sigmund Freud, Volume I (1886–1899): Pre-Psycho-Analytic Publications and Unpublished Drafts*. 1966. 103–114.
3. Freud, Sigmund. "The dynamics of transference." *The standard edition of the complete psychological works of Sigmund Freud, Volume XII (1911–1913): The case of Schreber, papers on technique and other works*. 1958. 97–108.
4. Lacan, Jacques. "Aggressivity in psychoanalysis." *Écrits: A selection* (1977): 8–29.
5. Samuels, Robert. "The Unconscious and the Primary Processes." *Freud for the Twenty-First Century*. Palgrave Pivot, Cham, 2019. 27–42.
6. Lacan, Jacques. "Some reflections on the ego." *International Journal of Psycho-Analysis* 34 (1953): 11–17.
7. Lacan, Jacques. *The four fundamental concepts of psycho-analysis*. Routledge, 2018.
8. Freud, Sigmund. *Totem and Taboo: Some Points of Agreement between the Mental Lives of Savages and Neurotics*. Routledge, 2013.
9. Grimaldi, William MA. *Aristotle, rhetoric I: A commentary*. Vol. 1. Fordham University Press, 1980.

10. Brooke, Robert. "Lacan, transference, and writing instruction." *College English* 49.6 (1987): 679–691.
11. Scalambrino, Frank. "Pre-Modern to Early Modern: From Mirror of God to Mirror of Nature." *Philosophical Principles of the History and Systems of Psychology*. Palgrave Macmillan, Cham, 2018. 89–128.
12. Samuels, Robert. *New media, cultural studies, and critical theory after post-modernism: Automodernity from Zizek to Laclau*. Springer, 2009.
13. Hegel, Georg Wilhelm Friedrich. *The phenomenology of mind*. Courier Corporation, 2012.
14. Freud, Sigmund. *The antithetical meaning of primal words*. Read Books Ltd., 2014.
15. Lacan, Jacques, and John Forrester. *The seminar of Jacques Lacan: Book II: The ego in Freud's theory and in the technique of psychoanalysis, 1954–1955*. Norton, 1988.
16. Lacan, Jacques. "The Mirror Stage as Formative of the Function of the I as Revealed in Psychoanalytic Experience 1." *Reading French Psychoanalysis*. Routledge, 2014. 97–104.
17. Lacan, Jacques. "Remarque sur le rapport de Daniel Lagache: 'Psychanalyse et structure de la personnalité'." *Écrits*. 1966. p. 647.
18. Freud, Sigmund. "A case of obsessional neurosis." *Standard edn* 10 (1909).
19. Lander, Christian. *Stuff white people like: A definitive guide to the unique taste of millions*. Random House, 2008.
20. Lander, Christian. *Stuff white people like: A definitive guide to the unique taste of millions*. Random House, 2008.
21. Freud, Sigmund. "Obsessive actions and religious practices." *The Standard Edition of the Complete Psychological Works of Sigmund Freud, Volume IX (1906–1908): Jensen's 'Gradiva' and Other Works*. 1959. 115–128.
22. Lacan, Jacques. "Aggressivity in psychoanalysis." *Écrits: A Selection* (1977): 8–29.
23. Leider, Robert J. "Analytic neutrality—a historical review." *Psychoanalytic Inquiry* 3.4 (1983): 665–674.
24. Siegel, Allen M. *Heinz Kohut and the Psychology of the Self*. Routledge, 2008.
25. Hamburg, Paul. "Interpretation and empathy: reading Lacan with Kohut." *International Journal of Psycho-Analysis* 72 (1991): 347–361.
26. Bloom, Harold. *The anxiety of influence: A theory of poetry*. Oxford University Press, USA, 1997.
27. Slavoj Žižek. *Less than nothing: Hegel and the shadow of dialectical materialism*. Verso Books, 2012.
28. Mills, Jon. "Lacan on paranoiac knowledge." *Psychoanalytic Psychology* 20.1 (2003): 30.

29. Janeck, Amy S., et al. "Too much thinking about thinking?: metacognitive differences in obsessive–compulsive disorder." *Journal of Anxiety Disorders* 17.2 (2003): 181–195.
30. Hamza, Agon, ed. *Repeating Žižek*. Duke University Press, 2015.
31. Sloterdijk, Peter. "Critique of cynical reason." (1988).
32. Leader, Darian. "Some notes on obsessional neurosis." *Lecture given at Leeds Metropolitan University, December* (1992).
33. Freud, Sigmund. *Totem and Taboo: Some Points of Agreement between the Mental Lives of Savages and Neurotics.* Routledge, 2013.
34. Samuels, Robert. *Psychoanalyzing the Politics of the New Brain Sciences.* Springer, 2017.
35. Lyotard, Jean-François. *The postmodern condition: A report on knowledge.* Vol. 10. U of Minnesota Press, 1984.
36. Žižek, Slavoj. *First as tragedy, then as farce.* Verso, 2009.
37. Samuels, Robert. *Educating inequality: beyond the political myths of higher education and the job market.* Routledge, 2017.
38. Arrow, Kenneth, Samuel Bowles, and Steven N. Durlauf, eds. *Meritocracy and economic inequality.* Princeton University Press, 2018.
39. Samuels, Robert. "Beyond Hillary Clinton: Obsessional Narcissism and the Failure of the Liberal Class." *Psychoanalyzing the Left and Right after Donald Trump.* Palgrave Macmillan, Cham, 2016. 31–59.
40. Rohde, David. "The Obama Doctrine." *Foreign Policy* 192 (2012): 65.
41. Gregory, Derek. "From a view to a kill: Drones and late modern war." *Theory, Culture & Society* 28.7–8 (2011): 188–215.
42. Domhoff, G. William. *Who rules America?: The triumph of the corporate rich.* McGraw-Hill Education, 2014.
43. Quadagno, Jill. "Right-wing conspiracy? Socialist plot? The origins of the patient protection and affordable care act." *Journal of Health Politics, Policy and Law* 39.1 (2014): 35–56.
44. Appelbaum, Binyamin. "Cautious moves on foreclosures haunting Obama." *New York Times* 19 (2012).
45. Moore, Wendy Leo, and Joyce M. Bell. "Embodying the White racial frame: The (in) significance of Barack Obama." *The Journal of Race & Policy* 6.1 (2010): 122.
46. Dutton, Donald G. "Tokenism, reverse discrimination, and egalitarianism in interracial behavior." *Journal of Social Issues* 32.2 (1976): 93–107.
47. Brooks, Rakim. "A Linked Fate: Barack Obama and Black America." *Dissent* 59.3 (2012): 42–45.

CHAPTER 5

Logos, Global Justice, and the Reality Principle

Abstract This chapter analyzes the relation between Freud's theory of the reality principle and the rhetorical category of logos. In drawing from Steven Pinker's *Enlightenment Now*, I argue that modern reason has played a key role in global progress. This privileging of reason is countered by Zizek's claim that it is impossible to apply logos in a neutral manner. Instead of opposing the Real and the Symbolic, Zizek locates conflict and contradiction in the Real itself.

Keywords Zizek • Lacan • Reality principle • Reason • Pinker • Science • Globalization

In the *Project for a Scientific Psychology*, Freud argues that as people develop, they must realize that they have to confront reality and use reason in order to distinguish the difference between their thoughts and their perceptions of the external world.[1] Since the unconscious treats thoughts as if they are reality, and the pleasure principle seeks to escape all conflict and tension, the development of the reality principle requires an overcoming of the "omnipotence of thought."[2] In other words, people have to accept the limits of their knowledge, and they have to be willing to accept the conflicted nature of the relation between the Real and the Symbolic. Following Kant, Freud posits that the Real is ultimately unknowable, but we can learn about our own thinking and the way our societies are

R. Samuels, *Zizek and the Rhetorical Unconscious*,
https://doi.org/10.1007/978-3-030-50910-1_5

structured. However, Freud also believes that this process of enlightenment is often blocked by transference and the belief in the Other as the one who always already knows the truth. The end of analysis then requires using logos as reason in order to move beyond ethos, pathos, and catharsis.[3]

This theory of individual development can be related to Steven Pinker's narrative of global progress in his *Enlightenment Now*.[4] According to Pinker, it is the combination of science, reason, and humanism that has led to a world where people live longer, healthier, wealthier, and freer lives. Although he spends very little time explaining what he means by reason (logos), we can follow Descartes in his defining reason as the ability to distinguish the true from the false through the impartial judgment of empirical evidence.[5] This definition relates to science and democracy because both modern institutions are centered on the relation between neutrality and empiricism. Just as we want our judges to examine evidence from a neutral perspective, we want scientists to pursue truth without self-interest. Of course, these are impossible ideals, but modern universality is centered on the continual effort to approach the ideal goal of neutrality. In fact, when the justice system is shown to be unjust, it is being judged against an ideal standard of universal equal treatment.

In terms of psychoanalysis, Freud discovered that when the analyst remains neutral, the patient becomes free to try to speak without self-censorship. In this process of free association, the subject learns to take a neutral perspective to his or her own discourse.[6] Neutrality then is the key invention of modernity, but it has now come under attack by postmodernists, who believe that since it is impossible to be perfectly neutral, this idea is used hide covert interests.[7] Instead of seeing neutrality as a bias against bias, postmodern critics on the Left posit that reason, universality, and impartiality are the products of white European males, and so they must be catering to the interest of this dominant class.[8] Just as feminists argue against Freud's conception of neutrality because it is impersonal, cold, and the result of his privileged position, postmodern thinkers on the Left believe that one can only speak from the position of one's particular position in the social hierarchy, and since women, people of color, and the poor embody their social position, they are not free to take on the neutral perspective of the unmarked universal modern subject of reason.[9]

One of the ironic effects of this discourse against reason, neutrality, and universality is that it can only be presented by using reason. In other words, even when people try to reject the value of using logos in order to communicate, they have to communicate their critique through this rhetorical mode. From this perspective Hegel was correct to stress that language always utilizes universal reason:

> Hegel was right to point out again and again that, when one talks, one always dwells in the universal—which means that, with its entry into language, the subject loses its roots in the concrete life world. To put it in more pathetic terms, the moment I start to talk, I am no longer the sensually concrete I, since I am caught up in an impersonal mechanism which always makes me say something different from what I wanted to say—as the early Lacan liked to say, I am not speaking, I am being spoken by language. This is one way to understand what Lacan called "symbolic castration": the price the subject pays for its "transubstantiation" from being the agent of a direct animal vitality to being a speaking subject whose identity is kept apart from the direct vitality of passions. (*Less Than Nothing* 197)

This notion of symbolic castration and the impersonal, mechanical aspects of language helps us to see the universal dimension of logos and the ways modernity introduces freedom and equality through the imposition of an impersonal, global order.

Reality and the Real

A key, then, to the application of reason in daily life and social institutions is the use of logos as a mode of artificial neutrality. In order to treat everyone with equal justice, we need to be neutral in relation to our self-interests and their differences. This neutral perspective has to be coupled with a use of empirical evidence that can be repeated and demonstrated to a universal audience.[10] It is vital to stress that universality and neutrality are not natural phenomena; rather, they represent human inventions derived from our use of language as a social means of communication. Yet, as Freud argued, language itself will not bring us to universal reason; rather, we have to learn through unpleasant experiences that we cannot think our way out of every conflict.

Instead of affirming the need for neutrality and the utilization of the reality principle, Zizek posits that neutrality is impossible: "The 'Real as impossible' is the cause of the impossibility of our ever attaining the 'neutral' non-perspectival view of the object" (*Less Than Nothing* 48). From this perspective, we can only have a skewed, partisan view of reality because the Real is impossible to know. On one level, this theory re-states Lacan's notion that since the Real is impossible to symbolize, all we can do is approach reality with incomplete knowledge. However, on another level, what Zizek is doing here is using the conflict between the Symbolic and the Real to posit that modern neutrality is impossible. One reason why he might be making this argument is that as far as I can tell, he never discusses the neutrality of the analyst in the process of psychoanalysis. In fact, he also appears to dismiss the possibility of free association in his own discourse because he claims that when he was in analysis, he made sure to plan out exactly what he was going to say. He also jokes that the reason why he does not stop talking when he makes a presentation is that he does not want to leave room for questions from the audience. In other terms, he wants to control the discourse so that he does not have to confront the criticism and unknowable desires of the audience.

Since logos is reliant on neutrality and empiricism, we have to understand how symbolic knowledge can approach reality from an impartial, universal perspective. Part of this theory relies on accepting the fundamental conflict between the Symbolic and the Real, since nothing lacks in the Real, and our sense of lack is only possible through Symbolic representation.[11] However, Zizek's big move is to argue that lack actually does exist in the real, and it is not our knowledge that is incomplete, but the Real itself is unfinished:

> It is Kant who goes only half-way in his destruction of metaphysics, still maintaining the reference to the Thing-in-itself as an external inaccessible entity, and Hegel is merely a radicalized Kant, who moves from our negative access to the Absolute to the Absolute itself as negativity. (*Less Than Nothing* 267)

This location of negativity in the Real projects the conflict between Symbolic knowledge and reality into a gap within reality itself. One of the problems with this theory is that it projects social conflicts into nature as if our social divisions are natural. This logic also makes logos impossible because it does not allow for neutrality and the acceptance of the limits of our knowledge in front of an unknowable real.

The science of logos and the discourse of psychoanalysis require a recognition that we can never overcome the differences between nature and culture, the individual and society, and language and the Real, but in Zizek's rhetoric, these differences are projected onto a Real that is shown to be lacking and divided:

> [T]he disparity between subject and substance is simultaneously the disparity of the substance with itself—or, to put it in Lacan's terms, disparity means that the lack of the subject is simultaneously the lack in the Other: subjectivity emerges when substance cannot achieve full identity with itself, when substance is in itself "barred," traversed by an immanent impossibility or antagonism. In short, the subject's epistemological ignorance, its failure to fully grasp the opposed substantial content, simultaneously indicates a limitation/failure/lack of the substantial content itself. (*Sex and the Failed Absolute* 21)

Instead of locating conflict within society or between society and the individual, Zizek believes that it is the substance of the natural Real that has been made to be incomplete and divided. One of the effects of this projection is that social conflicts are naturalized as nature is itself seen from the perspective of social division.[12]

This same process of projection is used to displace subjective and social conflict onto god in Zizek's post-religious use of Christianity:

> Therein also resides the key dimension of the theological revolution of Christianity: the alienation of man from god has to be projected/transferred back into god itself, as the alienation of god from itself (therein resides the speculative content of the notion of divine kenosis)—this is the Christian version of Hegel's insight into how the disparity of subject and substance implies the disparity of substance with regard to itself. (*Sex and the Failed Absolute* 21)

From Zizek's perspective, when Christ dies on the cross, it is god himself who dies, and therefore lack and division belong to the Absolute. Here we find a replacement of the psychoanalytic process with a cynical use of religion, since a key part of working through the transference in analysis is the discovery that the analyst does not know the subject's unconscious, and therefore this idealized Other is lacking.[13] However, Zizek argues that disparity is present in things themselves and not the relation between things and the subject.

Zizek then uses psychoanalytic rhetoric to repress psychoanalysis and project de-idealization and dis-identification onto a religious discourse in which he no longer believes:

> In Christianity, on the contrary, god falls from himself, he becomes a finite mortal human abandoned by god (in the figure of Christ and his lament on

> the cross, "My God, My God, why have you forsaken me?"), and man can only achieve unity with god by identifying with this god, god abandoned by himself. Therein resides the basic experience of Christianity: a Christian believer does not rejoin god directly, but only through the mediation of Christ—when Christ experiences himself as abandoned by god-father, a believer identifies his own alienation from god with the alienation of god (Christ) from himself, so that the very gap that separates him from god is what unites him with god. (*Sex and the Failed Absolute* 21)

Zizek's notion that it is god himself who vanishes on the cross is shared by very few actual Christians, and so this interpretation needs to be related to how he replaces psychoanalysis with religion and then voids religion of its central content.

One reason why Zizek's discourse may be so popular is that in the end, it is centered on a self-negating rhetoric, and therefore it does not require any subjective or social change.[14] By projecting social and subjective conflicts onto the Real, Zizek denies neutrality as he undermines logos, and thus his rhetoric works against psychoanalysis and the globalizing discourse of science and democracy. Since he does not believe that one should attempt to hold an impartial view of an unknowable Real, he does not accept that science is centered on the constant attempt to improve our approximation of reality. Likewise, modern global democracy is based on the application of universal human rights, which is always a work in progress. From this perspective, the universal is dynamic because it represents an impossible goal we can never fully attain but which we strive to achieve.[15]

Zizek and the Science of the Real

From the perspective of modern science, shared methods and symbolic systems of logic are utilized to represent a resistant Real in a self-critical manner. In other terms, we know that our representations of reality are only approximations, and so we need to remain critical of our own knowledge as we prioritize the Real through empirical reality testing.[16] In contrast, Zizek posits that it is not our knowledge that is limited and approximate; rather he argues that the Real is itself internally divided and lacking:

> Any project of general ontology outlining minimal formal conditions of all possible worlds is thus doomed to fail—but this does not condemn us to

> agnostic scepticism, since the shadow of uncertainty that falls upon every description of the real and confers on it an experimental character is a feature of the real-in-itself: the real-in-itself is traversed by a bar of impossibility and is "experimenting" with itself to construct flawed worlds. (26)

In this projection of experimentation onto nature, Zizek replaces logos with a new form of animism where things themselves take on the processes of human thought. We can understand this mode of projection onto the Real through Freud's notion that the first form of society was animistic because it was centered on the lack of difference between thoughts and perceptions.[17] As an example of the unconscious primary processes, animism projects our thoughts and feelings onto the external world, and like a hallucination, things become words and words become things. Since Freud draws an equivalency among animistic cultures, psychosis, infantile hallucination, and dreaming, his argument is that in the first stage of individual and social development, there is no distinction made between the inner and the outer world, and this distinction is only possible with the formation of the ego in the structure of narcissism.[18] Since the image in the mirror allows the subject to see a clear boundary between what is in the self and what is outside of the body-container, the internalization of the virtual self-image and body map allows for the break with the infantile projection of thought onto external reality.

As Freud outlines in *Totem and Taboo*, human civilization moves from animism to religion and then to science, and in this final stage, we realize the limitation of our own thoughts, and this helps us to separate our memories from our perceptions as we also stop relying on an idealized Other who already knows everything. Logos then is based on overcoming animism and religion, and from this perspective, we need to remain self-critical about our own thinking because it is the omnipotence of thoughts that causes animism and the infantile hallucination of reality. Given this historical structure outlined by Freud, we have to question why Zizek would return to a discourse of animism.

One possible reason for this projection of social and subjective conflict onto the Real is that our post-belief society continues to reiterate ideas and ideologies in which we no longer believe. In this type of zombie logic, we cannot escape from our past beliefs because as Freud argues, we are never able to forget anything in our unconscious, so old ideas never die; they just become repressed and covered over by new notions.[19] It is also important to realize that social systems often function by creating their own outside in a contained way. Thus in our highly mediated culture, we produce reality media as if this medium is no longer fake and scripted.[20] Cultures also produce their definitions of nature and the Real in order to offer a false escape from social control. The return to animism can therefore be read as a desire to escape from social control by maintaining a direct access to our thoughts in the Real.

From an ethical perspective, Freud posits that while the pleasure principle pushes us to escape from any feelings of guilt, shame, criticism, and responsibility, the reality principle as logos is centered on us accepting the fundamental conflicts between the individual and civilization.[21] As a discourse of radical self-honesty, psychoanalysis uses free association and the neutrality of the analyst to clear a space for a direct confrontation with inner and external reality.[22] However, with Zizek, he turns things on their head by constantly projecting these conflicts into the Real: "The old question 'How to derive Ought from Is?' (or: Meaning from Reality) can only be answered by way of locating an original cleft in the midst of the order of Being itself" (30). Instead of focusing on the conflicts between the Symbolic and the Real, culture and nature, and the social and the individual, Zizek locates these fundamental divisions in external reality, and here we return to the pure culture of the pleasure principle, since fault is not located in ourselves but in Being itself.[23]

The rhetorical combination of catharsis, pathos, and ethos can be seen in the way that Zizek turns to Hegel in order to reverse Marx and re-read Lacan. Since in the structure of transference and ethos, Hegel is the one who already knows the truth, Zizek's identification with this thinker helps him to overcome the pathos of conflict and achieve catharsis:

> The full step from Kant to Hegel goes beyond Fichte's or Schelling's direct identity of the real and the ideal, objective and subjective; it rather focuses on the question of how reality has to be structured so that symbolic order can emerge in it. Consequently, it posits that positive reality prior to the explosion of the Symbolic is not just that (a positive reality), that there is a crack in it, a proto-deontological tension or cleft: at its most basic, reality is not what is but what fails to be what it is, whose facticity is traversed by an impossibility. (32)

Although Lacan affirms that only language allows for lack and absence to enter into the world, Zizek turns to Hegel to argue that the lack in the Real allows for the emergence of the Symbolic order.[24] This argument moves away from the idea that nothing lacks in the Real because the Real is whatever it is. Once again, by locating negativity in the Real and not in the Symbolic or the subjective, Zizek removes conflict from the self and the social. Philosophy thus attains the Idealist goal of escaping from freedom and responsibility because everything is caused by a divided nature.

It has been my argument that global progress and psychoanalysis are predicated on going beyond catharsis by establishing logos in the form of the reality principle.[25] However, if we think about how communication and rhetoric actually function, we see that there is a need to combine together catharsis, ethos, pathos, and logos, since we cannot communicate without assuming that there is an Other who can use reason to understand what we are saying, and as a speaker, we have to maintain the illusion that we have ethos, and we know what we mean.[26] We also have to engage our audience through pathos and the promise of catharsis because pathos serves to gain the attention of the audience, while catharsis releases the pathos through the production of meaning and the satisfaction of understanding. From a pragmatic idealist rhetorical perspective, even though we can never know the truth or directly represent reality or fully understand someone else or even our own thoughts, we act as if these ideals are actualities. In fact, we can only examine the problems of language and communication by assuming an ideal order of reason, communication, and empiricism, and therefore any attempt to critique language by using language results in an ironic discourse where the medium being rejected is being used to make the rejection. This ironic discourse means that we cannot escape from logos, pathos, catharsis, and ethos because our only means of escape require all of these rhetorical modes.

Modernity and Separation

The modern solution to this need to combine logos, pathos, catharsis, and ethos is to use logic and critical introspection to separate these different aspects of communication.[27] Just as the human being has to learn how to separate thoughts from perception, science requires a distinction between thinking and the external world. In fact, in his text "negation," Freud argues that we have to learn how to mourn the loss of our desired objects, and this process requires giving up our initial investments through a process of working through.[28] Moreover, since we have a tendency to identify with the objects we lose, we also have to be able to separate from others without engaging in the process of identification. In the psychoanalytic process, this separation from the Other occurs with the working through of the transference, and here we see how psychoanalysis offers a unique method for developing individuation.[29]

The logic of separation can be seen in the way that modern societies separate church and state and divide the government into different branches (executive, judicial, and legislative). Modern states then need these separations to create a system of checks and balances, which work against the centralized control of premodern social systems.[30] While premodern societies are structured by binary oppositions and social hierarchies, modernity relies on separation and universal equality.[31]

Not only is modernity founded on the separation of the premodern order of religion from modern science, but also within modernity, we find the separation of democracy and capitalism on the one hand, and capitalism and science on the other hand.[32] It is in fact this relation between capitalism and democracy that poses the biggest problem for contemporary global theorists like Zizek:

> if Europe is in gradual decay, what is replacing its hegemony? The answer is: "capitalism with Asian values" (which, of course, has nothing to do with Asian people and everything to do with the clear and present tendency of contemporary capitalism as such to suspend democracy). From Marx on, the truly radical Left was never simply "progressist". It was always obsessed by the question: what is the price of progress? Marx was fascinated by capitalism, by the unheard-of productivity it unleashed; it was just that he insisted that this very success engenders antagonisms. And we should do the same with the progress of global capitalism today: keep in view its dark underside, which is fomenting revolts. (*Trouble in Paradise: From the End of History to the End of Capitalism* 23–24)[33]

As one of the key modern institutions fueling global progress, capitalism needs to be contained by democratic law and regulation because of its ability to undermine any stable structures; however, as Zizek highlights, we are currently witnessing the ability of capitalism to threaten democracy and to couple itself with premodern centralized authority.

The example of China raises many difficult problems for our understanding of modernity because instead of democracy, science, and capitalism developing together, we now see many examples of democracy being subverted by both capitalism and a return to premodern social hierarchies:

> What all this implies is that today's conservatives are not really conservative. While fully endorsing capitalism's continuous self-revolutionizing, they just want to make it more efficient by supplementing it with some traditional institutions (religion, for instance) to constrain its destructive consequences for social life and to maintain social cohesion. Today, a true conservative is the one who fully admits the antagonisms and deadlocks of global capitalisms, the one who rejects simple progressivism, and who is attentive to the dark obverse of progress. In this sense, only a radical Leftist can be today a true conservative. (24)

In this ironic reversal, Zizek posits that the Left must reject progressivism and take on a more conservative perspective in order to critique the dark side of capitalism and progress. Here we see Zizek turning against global progress because of the failure of the state to regulate the excesses of capitalism.

In contrast to Zizek, Pinker highlights how the combination of state planning and capitalism in China has helped to remove millions of people out of dire poverty as it has contributed to the expansion of global lifespans.[34] On one level, China does lack many aspects of a democratic state, but if we center our understanding of modern democracy on the institution of universal law, China can be seen in a much more mixed light.[35] After all, as Mariana Mazzucota highlights in *The Entrepreneurial State*, what has looked like pure free market capitalism in the West has most often been a mix of governmental support and private business, and so the binary opposition between capitalism and the state is often called into question.[36] For instance, virtually every technology on the iPhone was first developed by the US defense and space programs, and most of these technologies were tested at federally funded universities. While the Left often runs against capitalism and the Right now runs against government, what has helped to usher in the age of global progress is often a combination of capitalism and the government.

Although the modern state seeks to separate capitalism and democracy, this separation also entails a constant dialectical relationship between these different modern systems. In fact, Zizek highlights how one problem facing global progress is that with each increase in the standard of living, people's expectations also rise:

> Chinese Communists are right to be in a panic: precisely because, on average, Chinese are now living considerably better than forty years ago, but the

> social antagonisms (between the newly rich and the rest) have exploded, plus people's expectations are now generally much higher. That's the problem with development and progress: they are always uneven, they give birth to new instabilities and antagonisms, they generate new expectations which cannot be met. (*Trouble in Paradise* 24–25)

Of course, economic and social development is uneven and full of conflicts, but we need to recognize that the path of history has moved in one direction and that is toward greater life expectancy, greater freedom, and greater prosperity.[37] One issue is that very few people know about these positive transformations, and so they do not see what has worked in the past and what might continue to work in the future.

For many critics on the Left, it is simply naïve and wrong to believe that the combination of capitalism, democracy, and science has led on average to a tremendous improvement in the living standards of people all over the world. As Zizek posits, these modern institutions fueling global progress are undermined by the constant threats posed by the insanity of capitalism: "When we stick to such a purity of market capitalism, dismissing its failures as accidental mishaps, we end up in a naive progressivism that ignores the mad dance of the opposites" (25–26). The problem with this analysis of our current condition is that it uses the libertarian ideology of the totally free market to represent capitalism as a purely unconstrained system of mad destruction.[38] Once again, in order to generate pathos, Zizek employs an extremist rhetoric that blinds us from seeing a much more balanced representation of the overall trends of globalization.[39]

Never have more people been gainfully employed around the world, and never have they had more opportunities to remove themselves from dire poverty, but from Zizek's perspective, global capitalism has to be seen primarily through the pathos of risks and threats:

> in the ongoing process of capitalist globalization, the category of the unemployed has acquired a new quality beyond the classic notion of the "reserve army of labour". One should consider, in terms of the category of unemployment, "those massive populations around the world who have, as it were, 'dropped out of history', who have been deliberately excluded from the modernizing projects of First World capitalism and written off as hopeless or terminal cases": so-called "failed states" (Congo, Somalia), victims of famine or ecological disasters, caught in pseudo-archaic "ethnic hatreds", objects of philanthropy and NGOs or (often the same people) of the "war on terror". The category of the unemployed should thus be expanded to

> encompass the wide span of population from the temporarily unemployed, through the no-longer-employable and permanently unemployed, up to people living in slums and other types of ghettos (all those often dismissed by Marx himself as "lumpen-proletarians") and, finally, entire areas, populations or states excluded from the global capitalist process, like the blank spaces in ancient maps. (26–27)

Although it is vital to address the different issues Zizek has articulated, the listing of these problems should not blind us from the fact that dire global poverty has been reduced by 90% in the last 200 years, and global lifespans have doubled in the last 200 years.[40] Much of this progress can be related to the mixture of global capitalism, science, and democracy, and so it is important to recognize the incredible advances that this modern institution has helped to produce.

Driving much of Zizek's rhetorical use of pathos while describing global capitalism is his belief that "the immanent logic of market relations ... tends towards exploitation and destabilizing excesses" (28). In other words, global capitalism must result in an undermining of human life and stability because it is driven by an irrational logic. This view neglects the fact that for much of human history, most people in the world lived short, brutish lives, and it is only with modernity that this state has been transformed.[41]

Of course, a very real problem is that as the global South and East continues reap the benefits of economic prosperity, workers in the developed West have seen some of their jobs eliminated.[42] This global market for labor has resulted in a backlash in many Western democracies as immigrants and global trade deals have been blamed for job loss. The Western political reaction to globalization can in part be traced to the failure of social welfare programs to help out displaced workers, but a larger problem is that politicians on the Left have also attacked globalization as the cause of all of our economic misery. The Right and the Left have therefore have taken a stand against globalization in favor of an outdated model of nationalism. In fact, the one thing that Donald Trump and Bernie Sanders appeared to agree on is that globalization and global trade deals are destroying the American economy.[43] Instead of the Left realizing the importance of global gains in life expectancy and the reduction of dire poverty, the focus has been on the segment of the population that has lost jobs to automation and global outsourcing. These very real problems need to be addressed in a direct manner, but when globalization is blamed, the only solution is destructive nationalism.

Zizek's demonization of global capitalism is coupled with an attack on modern liberal democracy, which he sees as undermining any real solution to our current conflicts.[44] From his perspective, the fundamental battle between premodern social hierarchies and modern equality and freedom is a false opposition:

> When we hear today's politicians or ideologists offering us a choice between liberal freedom and fundamentalist oppression, and triumphantly asking a (purely rhetorical) question "Do you want women to be excluded from public life and deprived of their elementary rights? Do you want everyone who mocks religion to be punished by death?", what should make us suspicious is the very self-evidence of the answer—who would ever want that? The problem is that such a simplistic liberal universalism lost its innocence long ago. This is why, for a true Leftist, the conflict between liberal permissiveness and fundamentalism is ultimately a false conflict—a vicious cycle of two poles generating and presupposing each other. (114–15)

According to Zizek's logic, modern democratic human rights produce premodern fundamentalisms in a false conflict, but this argument relies on discrediting the value of liberal universalism and equated it with what it is trying to replace. Instead of recognizing the incredible growth in protected human rights, Zizek seeks to blame the solution for the problem in order to clear the space for a Leftist alternative.

As I discussed in the previous chapter, one of the main problems of contemporary liberals is that they are often so focused on looking good and having good intentions that they are unable to examine some of the harm caused by their own policies.[45] Moreover, these narcissistic liberals are fearful of the Left because they do not want to see any radical change to the status quo. However, it would be wrong to equate contemporary liberals with modern liberalism, since their cynical conformity and defensiveness prevents them from using reason and evidence in their public policy and political ideology. However, for Zizek, the real problem with liberals is that they do not critique modern liberal democracy and capitalism:

> One should take a Hegelian step back and question the very measure from which fundamentalism appears in all its horror. What Max Horkheimer said about Fascism and capitalism back in the 1930s (those who do not want to

> talk critically about capitalism should also keep quiet about Fascism) can be applied to today's fundamentalism: those who do not want to talk (critically) about liberal democracy and its noble principles should also keep quiet about religious fundamentalism. (115)

Zizek argues that since liberals are not critically examining liberal democracy and capitalism, they should also stop attacking religious fundamentalism, but this line of analysis implies that there is a moral equivalence between premodern fundamentalism and the modern principles of the Enlightenment.

In Zizek's desire to sustain a Leftist focus on class war, he goes as far as trying to show how extreme religious fundamentalism and terrorism may actually be a Leftist project:

> The Taliban are regularly presented as a fundamentalist Islamist group enforcing its rule with terror—however, when, in the spring of 2009, they took over the Swat valley in Pakistan, the New York Times reported that they engineered "a class revolt that exploits profound fissures between a small group of wealthy landlords and their landless tenants". The ideological bias of the New York Times article is discernible in how it speaks of the Taliban's "ability to exploit class divisions", as if the Taliban's "true" agenda is elsewhere—in religious fundamentalism—and they are merely "taking advantage" of the plight of the poor landless farmers. (116)

It should be clear to Zizek that the Taliban represent a fundamentalist return to the premodern discourse of the master and that they are only using class conflict to spread their ideology and power, but the reason he may not want to say this is that his transference to Hegel and Marx forces him to reject liberal democracy and seek out a Leftist agenda. One of the main reasons why he mis-reads these political movements is that he believes the Left does not have its own agenda, but he misrecognizes why this is the case.

I have been arguing that the real failure of the Left is its inability to embrace globalization and the modern institutions of capitalism, science, and democracy; instead, the Left is fragmented among groups focusing on race, gender, sexuality, and capitalism. Furthermore, critics like Zizek do not see how identity politics is necessary for expanding modern universality, but the problems ensue when it becomes fixated on identity and fails to unify around the goal of equality.[46] Yet, for Zizek, the main problem is that when the Left does not concentrate on resolving class conflict, it opens up the door for the Right to address this issue: "if moderate liberal forces continue to ignore the radical Left, they will generate an insurmountable fundamentalist wave" (116). In other words, fundamentalism and reactionary Right-wing politics are caused by the liberal rejection of the Left. This analysis is very seductive, but it is based on the misguided notion that premodern religious fundamentalism is a failed form of the Left critique of modern capitalism. One problem with this perspective is that religion predates modern capitalism, and it is modernity itself that has posed the central threat to all premodern ideologies and social systems. As a discourse that does not recognize any borders, beliefs, or limits, modern capitalism does indeed melt away all premodern solid traditions.[47] On one level, Zizek does recognize this power of modernity, but due to his need to demonize capitalism as the cause of the world ills, he has to reject one of the driving force of the modern globalizing world.

Zizek posits that the only hope for liberals is to align with the radical Left, but what liberals are afraid of is the global demand for social justice:

> In order for the key liberal legacy to survive, liberals need the fraternal help of the radical Left. Although (almost) everyone enthusiastically supported these democratic explosions, there is a hidden struggle for their appropriation. Official circles and most of the media in the West celebrate them as the same thing as the "pro-democracy" velvet revolutions in Eastern Europe: a desire for Western liberal democracy, a desire to become like the West. This is why uneasiness arises when one sees that there is something else at work in these protests: a demand for social justice. (117)

Since Zizek thinks that the only way to pursue justice is through class conflict, he undervalues the power of the modern global institution of universal human rights.

A clear demonstration of Zizek's distorted view of our globalized world can be seen in the following passage:

> [I]n the last decades we witnessed a whole series of emancipatory popular explosions which were re-appropriated by the global capitalist order, either in its liberal form (from South Africa to the Philippines) or in its fundamentalist form (Iran). We should not forget that none of the Arab countries where popular uprisings have happened is formally democratic: they were all more or less authoritarian, so that the demand for social and economic justice was spontaneously integrated into the demand for democracy, as if pov-

erty was the result of the greed and corruption of those in power, and it was enough to get rid of them. What happens is that we get democracy, but poverty remains—what to do then? (117)

Zizek's analysis here relies on seeing global capitalism as the only cause of social problems so that even if people demand more democracy, they will still fail to address poverty. On one level, this analysis is true because democratic law does not in itself reduce economic deprivation, but it is in part the spread of global capitalism that has helped to reduce dire poverty throughout the world.[48] Of course, this economic progress is very uneven and does not move in a straight line, but there has been constant progress, and it is mostly due to global economic integration and the move toward universal human rights and science-based discoveries in health and technology.

The key problem that I am pointing to here is that there is not a political group centered on promoting globalization and democratic law; instead, we have the Left and the Right attacking globalization, while the liberal center attacks the Left and the Right.[49] A main reason for this problem is that international politics are still framed in terms of nations and nationalism, and so it is hard to take on a global perspective. For Zizek, the fantasy that he constantly returns to is one of a new form of Communism without the horrors of totalitarianism, but this return to a dying ideology blinds him from seeing how progress and solidarity actually function:

> It is true that there is something of an imaginary unity in the first climax of the revolt, when all groups are united in the rejection of the tyrant. However, there is more in this unity than imaginary ideological illusion—every radical revolt by definition contains a Communist dimension, a dream of solidarity and egalitarian justice that reaches beyond the narrow sphere of politics into economy, private life and culture, permeating the entire social edifice. (117)

While Zizek believes that social solidarity is equal to Communism, I have been arguing that global human rights are shaped by the modern discourses of universality and neutral judgment.

As Zizek's own example of Martin Luther King Jr. reveals, social progress often occurs when a postmodern social movement focused on an individual group's call for justice transforms into a modern discourse of universal equality: "Let us return to Martin Luther King: to put it in Badiou's terms, King followed the 'axiom of equality' well beyond the topic of racial segregation, and his readiness to pursue that work makes him a true fighter for emancipation" (118). What Zizek and others constantly fail to understand is that there is an inherent conflict between what motivates a social movement and the ultimate goal of justice and equality: one has to begin with building solidarity through a shared victim identity, but in order to attain justice, this identity has to be replaced by the impersonal law. Here we see how political progress is similar to psychoanalysis; in both cases, you need to start with the pathos of victim identity and identification, but the goal is to use modern logos to affirm universal neutrality.[50]

What often blocks this transformation from postmodern identity politics to modern equality is the ethos of political ideology in the form of the cynical conformity to dead ideas and the transference to dead ideals. In Zizek's case, it is clear that his idealization of the idea of Communism blinds him from taking a modern view of the political world:

> In authoritarian right-wing countries, all those who fight (no matter how peacefully) for democracy, freedom, justice and other liberal goals, were (and in some cases still are) denounced as Communists or as gullible ignorants manipulated by Communists, the highest enemy of the state. The elementary liberal reaction to such accusations is denial: "No, we are just sincere fighters for freedom and democracy, and since you (those in power) are really against freedom and democracy but are not ready to admit this publicly, you accuse us nonsensically of Communism." But what if the Rightists who denounce those who fight for freedom as undercover Communists are ultimately right? What if, in a situation of intense emancipatory struggle when opportunists are afraid of the explosion of popular rage and tend to enact a compromise with the Right in power, the Communists are the only ones who unconditionally defend freedom and justice against authoritarian power? So, after rejecting such accusations ("Me, a Communist? Are you crazy? We are just consequent liberals!"), a moment arrives when the only consequent reaction is to accept the accusations: "YES, so what, we are Communists, you pushed us into it!" (118–19)

Since Zizek did grow up under Communist rule, we can read the passage above as indicting one of the reasons he provokes people by calling himself a Communist.[51] From his perspective, the only people who do not compromise and who demand social justice and freedom are those who are called Communists, and so he has embraced this term, but clearly, Communism is not the historical path to social equality and justice. Zizek simply refuses to admit that it is a mix of modern capitalism, democracy, and science that has led to global human rights and the extension of human lifespans.

In the conclusion, I will further examine Zizek's use of the term Communism and offer an alternative view of the future of global politics. By returning to the modern rhetoric of logos, I hope to show how we can move beyond the ethos of old ideas and the catharsis of guilt and shame. What we need to do is to do is focus on logos in the form of universal justice, scientific advancement, and global interdependence. However, part of modern reason requires the need for critical introspection. For instance, throughout this book, I have perhaps idealized Freud as the one who already always knows. This use of ethos reveals why it is impossible to communicate without the transference to an authority embodying ethos as the guarantee of truth. The need to rely on a previous source of knowledge points to the ways we cannot escape this aspect of rhetoric, and in the case of my use of Freud, I position him as the ego ideal, and then I judge my discourse from his perspective. To overcome this idealizing transference, it is essential to remain critical of Freud's tendency to imagine a future where biology will answer all of our questions. In fact, the recent fields of neuroscience and evolutionary psychology point to this desire to ground all mental functions in a natural order. We therefore need to remain critical of the naturalization of social and psychological processes.

Notes

1. Freud, Sigmund. "Project for a scientific psychology (1950 [1895])." *The Standard Edition of the Complete Psychological Works of Sigmund Freud, Volume I (1886–1899): Pre-Psycho-Analytic Publications and Unpublished Drafts.* 1966. 281–391.
2. Freud, Sigmund. *Totem and Taboo: Some Points of Agreement between the Mental Lives of Savages and Neurotics.* Routledge, 2013.
3. Samuels, Robert. "The Resistances to Psychoanalysis and Global Progress." *Freud for the Twenty-First Century.* Palgrave Pivot, Cham, 2019. 53–67.
4. Pinker, Steven. *Enlightenment now: The case for reason, science, humanism, and progress.* Penguin, 2018.
5. Descartes, René, and Donald A. Cress. *Discourse on method.* Hackett Publishing, 1998.
6. Greenberg, Jay R. "Theoretical models and the analyst's neutrality." *Contemporary Psychoanalysis* 22.1 (1986): 87–106.
7. Crittenden, Paul J. "Neutrality in education." *Educational Philosophy and Theory* 12.1 (1980): 1–18.

8. Inoue, Asao B. *Antiracist writing assessment ecologies: Teaching and assessing writing for a socially just future*. WAC Clearinghouse, 2015.
9. Minow, Martha. "Beyond Universality." *U. Chi. Legal F.* (1989): 115.
10. Hiller, Harry H. "Universality of science and the question of national sociologies." *American Sociologist* 14.3 (1979).
11. Lacan, Jacques. *The Seminar of Jacques Lacan: The Ego in Freud's Theory and in the Technique of Psychoanalysis 1954–1955/Translated by Sylvana Tomaselli; with Notes by John Forrester*. WW Norton, 2011.
12. Samuels, Robert. *Psychoanalyzing the Politics of the New Brain Sciences*. Springer, 2017.
13. Lacan, Jacques. "The seminar of Jacques Lacan: Book VIII: Transference: 1960–1961." (2011).
14. Samuels, Robert. "Žižek's Rhetorical Matrix: The Symptomatic Enjoyment of Postmodern Academic Writing." *JAC* (2002): 327–354.
15. Cerna, Christina M. "Universality of human rights and cultural diversity: implementation of human rights in different socio-cultural contexts." *Hum. Rts. Q.* 16 (1994): 740.
16. White, Halbert. *Artificial neural networks: approximation and learning theory*. Blackwell Publishers, Inc., 1992.
17. Freud, Sigmund. "Animism, magic and the omnipotence of thoughts." *Totem and Taboo* (1913): 75–99.
18. Freud, Sigmund. "On narcissism: An introduction." *The Standard Edition of the Complete Psychological Works of Sigmund Freud, Volume XIV (1914–1916): On the History of the Psycho-Analytic Movement, Papers on Metapsychology and Other Works*. 1957. 67–102.
19. Freud, Sigmund. "Formulations on the two principles of mental functioning." *The Standard Edition of the Complete Psychological Works of Sigmund Freud, Volume XII (1911–1913): The Case of Schreber, Papers on Technique and Other Works*. 1958. 213–226.
20. Gamson, William A., et al. "Media images and the social construction of reality." *Annual Review of Sociology* 18.1 (1992): 373–393.
21. Samuels, Robert. "Science and the Reality Principle." *Freud for the Twenty-First Century*. Palgrave Pivot, Cham, 2019. 5–16.
22. Wallwork, Ernest. *Psychoanalysis and ethics*. Yale University Press, 1994.
23. Shepherdson, Charles. "History and the real: Foucault with Lacan." *Postmodern Culture* 5.2 (1995).
24. Samuels, Robert. *Between philosophy and psychoanalysis: Lacan's reconstruction of Freud*. Routledge, 2014.
25. Samuels, Robert. "The Resistances to Psychoanalysis and Global Progress." *Freud for the Twenty-First Century*. Palgrave Pivot, Cham, 2019. 53–67.
26. Habermas, Jurgen, Axel Honneth, and Hans Joas. *Communicative action*. Vol. 1. 1991.

27. Habermas, Jürgen. "Modernity—an incomplete project." *Postmodernism: A reader* (1993): 98–109.
28. Freud, Sigmund. "Negation." *International Journal of Psycho-Analysis* 6 (1925): 367–371.
29. Bracher, Mark. "How analysis cures according to Lacan." *The subject of Lacan: A Lacanian reader for psychologists* (2000): 189–208.
30. Mendieta, Eduardo. "Rationalization, modernity and secularization." *Jurgen Habermas.* Routledge, 2014. 236–252.
31. Jowett, Benjamin, ed. *The politics of Aristotle.* Vol. 1. Clarendon Press, 1885.
32. Wagner, Peter. "Modernity, capitalism and critique." *Thesis Eleven* 66.1 (2001): 1–31.
33. Žižek, Slavoj. *Trouble in paradise: From the end of history to the end of capitalism.* Melville house, 2015.
34. Pinker, Steven. *Enlightenment now: The case for reason, science, humanism, and progress.* Penguin, 2018.
35. Shambaugh, David L. *China goes global: The partial power.* Vol. 111. Oxford: Oxford University Press, 2013.
36. Mazzucato, Mariana. *The entrepreneurial state: Debunking public* vs. *private sector myths.* Vol. 1. Anthem Press, 2015.
37. Brynjolfsson, Erik, and Andrew McAfee. "Jobs, productivity and the great decoupling." *The New York Times* 11 (2012): 2012.
38. Tilman, Rick. *Ideology and utopia in the social philosophy of the libertarian economists.* Westport, CT: Greenwood Press, 2001.
39. International Labour Office. *World employment and social outlook: trends 2015.* Geneva: International Labour Organization, 2015.
40. Pinker, Steven. *Enlightenment now: The case for reason, science, humanism, and progress.* Penguin, 2018.
41. Ridley, Matt. "The rational optimist: How prosperity evolves." *Brock Education: A Journal of Educational Research and Practice* 21.2 (2012).
42. Brand, Jennie E. "The far-reaching impact of job loss and unemployment." *Annual Review of Sociology* 41 (2015).
43. Samuels, Robert. "Trump and Sanders on the Couch: Neoliberal Populism on the Left and the Right." *Psychoanalyzing the Left and Right after Donald Trump.* Palgrave Macmillan, Cham, 2016. 61–76.
44. Dean, Jodi. "Zizek against democracy." *Law, Culture and the Humanities* 1.2 (2005): 154–177.
45. Samuels, Robert. "(Liberal) Narcissism." *Routledge Handbook of Psychoanalytic Political Theory.* Routledge, 2019. 151–161.
46. Hobsbawm, Eric. "Identity politics and the left." *New Left Review* (1996): 38–47.
47. Marx, Karl, and Friedrich Engels. *The communist manifesto.* Penguin, 2002.

48. Shoaf Kozak, Rebecca, Margaret Lombe, and Katia Miller. "Global poverty and hunger: An assessment of Millennium Development Goal# 1." *Journal of Poverty* 16.4 (2012): 469–485.
49. Samuels, Robert. "The Resistances to Psychoanalysis and Global Progress." *Freud for the Twenty-First Century*. Palgrave Pivot, Cham, 2019. 53–67.
50. Samuels, Robert. "Global Solidarity and Global Government: The Universal Subject of Psychoanalysis and Democracy." *Psychoanalyzing the Left and Right after Donald Trump*. Palgrave Macmillan, Cham, 2016. 77–101.
51. McMillan, Chris. *Žižek and communist strategy*. Edinburgh University Press, 2013.

CHAPTER 6

Conclusion: Communism or Commonism?

Abstract In the conclusion, I will examine Zizek's use of the term Communism and offer an alternative view of the future of global politics. By returning to the modern rhetoric of logos, I hope to show how we can move beyond the ethos of old ideas and the catharsis of guilt and shame. What we need to do is to focus on logos in the form of universal justice, scientific advancement, and global interdependence.

Keywords Zizek • Globalization • Universality • Logos • Science • Commonism

As Zizek rightly points out, our most threatening problems today all are global in nature and will require some form of global response.[1] After all, you cannot fight climate change as an individual country because we all share the same environment. Moreover, with the global spread of labor and production, national laws are unable to regulate workers' rights or collect taxes from multinational corporations or wealthy individuals.[2] We are also witnessing constant problems caused by global travel and migration, such as the spread of disease or the distribution of illegal products. The only solution is therefore a global solution, and this will require moving away from the current nation-based political structure. In fact, we can see Brexit and Trump as examples of the last resistances of a dying nationalist order.[3]

R. Samuels, *Zizek and the Rhetorical Unconscious*,
https://doi.org/10.1007/978-3-030-50910-1_6

To move to this new global system, we have to overcome our unconscious investments in dead ideas as we turn to modern science and democracy to base public policy on logos and not on pathos, catharsis, and ethos.[4] In this context, it is interesting to see why Zizek believes that the solution to these global problems relies on returning to the idea of Communism. In order to make this argument, he begins by focusing on what he calls the four main antagonisms of the current globalized world:

> They concern (1) the commons of culture in the broadest sense, of "immaterial" capital: the immediately socialized forms of "cognitive" capital, primarily language, our means of communication and education, not to mention the financial sphere with the absurd consequences of uncontrolled virtual money circulation; (2) the commons of external nature, threatened by human pollution: all particular dangers – global warming, dying of the oceans, etc. – are aspects of a derailment of the entire life reproduction system on earth; (3) the commons of internal nature (the biogenetic inheritance of humanity): with new biogenetic technology, the creation of a New Man in the literal sense of changing human nature becomes a realistic prospect; and, last but not least, (4) the commons of humanity itself, of the shared social and political space: the more capitalism gets global, the more new walls and apartheids are emerging, separating those who are IN from those who are OUT. (*The Courage of Hopelessness* 6)

The basic issues that Zizek focuses on here are global financial capitalism, climate change, biogenetics, and social segregation. All of these important problems threaten our global progress, and all of them must be countered by some type of international law and global coordination.[5] However, Zizek's curious solution to these problems is to return to the ideology of Communism: "It is this reference to 'commons' that justifies the resuscitation of the notion of communism: it enables us to see the progressive 'enclosure' of the commons as a process of proletarianization of those who are thereby excluded from the very substance of their lives" (6). The first way that he tries to re-activate Communism is by connecting it to the notion of the commons; just as our common space has been privatized through modern capitalism, Zizek posits that our common humanity has been taken over by making us all proletariats who have lost the control over our own lives.

The underlying idea here is that we once all shared ownership over our environment, our bodies, and our relationship to other people, but now all of these things we held in common have been taken from us through the process of transforming everything into private property controlled by multinational corporations. This extremist view generates a lot of pathos, but is it true? Of course, on one level, we are seeing capitalism spread to all parts of the world and to many aspects of our lives, but we need to ask if we ever had control over these common properties. Clearly, we never controlled the environment or our own genetics, but is the new stage of global capitalism threatening to control every aspect of our lives? Furthermore, is the only solution to eliminate private property and have the people directly own everything in common?

The question that the Communists always run into is who will organize and coordinate the people; in other terms, will the state simply wither away because it is unneeded? Everything in our history tells us that the centralized state will only become more powerful when people believe that private property belongs to everyone.[6] Yet, Zizek wants to hold onto the idea of Communism as the solution to our global problems:

> Only the fourth antagonism, the reference to the excluded, justifies the term communism: the first three effectively concern questions of humanity's economic, anthropological, even physical, survival, while the fourth one is ultimately a question of justice. But here we stumble upon the old boring question of the relationship between socialism and communism: why call the goal of a radical emancipatory movement communism? In the Marxist tradition, socialism was conceptualized as the (in)famous lower stage of communism, so that the "progress" was supposed to run from socialism to communism. (No wonder that, with regard to the sad reality of life under "really existing socialism", jokes abounded like the well-known one from the Soviet Union where a group of people in Moscow are reading a big propaganda poster which says: "In twenty years, we will live in full communism!" One of the people starts to laugh and jump with pleasure and joy, and when others ask him why, he replies: "I have cancer, I will be dead for sure in twenty years!") But the reality was different; most socialist countries, rather, began with some version of primitive but radical communism (the Soviet Union in 1918–20, etc.), and then, in order to survive, they had to "regress" and make compromises with the old society – so the line of development ran from communism to socialism (which combined the old and the new). The worst thing we can do today is to drop the name "communism" and advocate a watered-down version of "democratic socialism". The task confronting us today is precisely the reinvention of communism, a radical change that moves well beyond some vague notion of social solidarity.

> Insofar as, in the course of the historical process of change, its goal itself should be redefined, we can say that "communism" is to be reinvented as the name for what emerges as the goal after the failure of socialism. (6)

This long passage embodies all of the different modes of unconscious rhetoric in Zizek's discourse. On one level, he returns to the discredited ethos of Communism as a cynical conformity to a dead ideal. This use of a provocative signifier opens him up to criticism that he can then use to show how he is a victim because he is being attacked. Furthermore, the pathos generated from this victim identification is then coupled with the cathartic use of a joke to create enjoyment for his audience and separate his discourse from any responsibility. Instead of focusing on the empirical evidence concerning the way Communism has resulted in a lack of justice, equality, and freedom, he holds onto this label derived from his childhood in a transferential relationship.[7] By denying the logos of the facts and the role played by modern liberal democracy in extending global human rights and freedom, he repeats a failed revolution from a position of distance.

The pathos and defensiveness of his position is clearly stated when he details some of the ways that he has been critiqued for his discourse:

> This approach to communism (expounded in many recent books of mine) has lately been submitted to a series of criticisms – basically, my critics identify five principal sins: my (openly admitted) eurocentrism, i.e., my insistence on the European roots of the project of universal emancipation; my rejection of the Greek Left Platform proposal to risk a more radical measure (Grexit, etc.) after the victory of the Syriza government at the referendum; my critique of the elevation of refugees and migrants into a new form of global proletariat and my insistence on the problems of cultural identity; my doubts about some ideological components of the LGBT+ movement; and, last but not least, my "support" for the "fascist" Donald Trump. As expected, all these reproaches are combined into the thesis that I am effectively a homophobic eurocentrist racist who opposes any authentic radical measure. (6)

Since my own work can be accused of Eurocentrism, I want to stress that the model of modernity and globalization I am endorsing represents a bias against bias in the effort to use neutrality and universal equality. While it is true that these ideas gained the most traction in modern Europe, it should be clear that universality counters any specific groups interests.

Furthermore, the evidence of global progress shows that people from many different cultures have benefited from this philosophy that supports modern science and democracy. It should also be stressed that when minorities seek justice, they desire to be included into modern universal human rights. However, Zizek's rhetorical strategy of creating pathos by provoking his audience should be recognized as a self-defeating discourse.

What global philosophy needs to do is to promote the importance of modern neutrality and universality as it remains self-critical concerning the use of catharsis, pathos, and ethos as unconscious defense mechanisms. Although it is important to recognize the need for postmodern social movements to expand the universal sphere of democratic rights, we have to acknowledge the fundamental conflict between postmodern pathos and modern logos. Since the universal is always changing, we should think about a version of Hegel's dialectic that is dynamic and does not seek to resolve every opposition and conflict on an Imaginary level. This discourse also should work through our dependency on an omniscient Other who is posited as the one who already knows the truth.

As Freud's theory of the reality principle posits, global philosophy is predicated on taking an impartial view of empirical evidence by separating our thoughts from our perceptions of external reality. This process requires admitting that our knowledge will always be incomplete, and the best we can do is to approximate our approach to the Real by using shared Symbolic methods and logic. Since all acts of communication require the use of ethos, logos, pathos, and catharsis, we have to develop a language to address these different unconscious rhetorical modes. My hope is that this book has helped to articulate some of the ways we can examine our own unconscious processes in a rational manner.

Notes

1. Stiglitz, Joseph, and Robert M. Pike. "Globalization and its Discontents." *Canadian Journal of Sociology* 29.2 (2004): 321.
2. Freeman, Richard. "The great doubling: The challenge of the new global labor market." *Draft, Harvard University* (2006).
3. Gusterson, Hugh. "From Brexit to Trump: Anthropology and the rise of nationalist populism." *American Ethnologist* 44.2 (2017): 209–214.
4. Young, Ken, et al. "Social science and the evidence-based policy movement." *Social Policy and Society* 1.3 (2002): 215–224.

5. Stiglitz, Joseph, and Robert M. Pike. "Globalization and its Discontents." *Canadian Journal of Sociology* 29.2 (2004): 321.
6. Pipes, Richard. *Communism: A history*. Vol. 7. Modern Library Chronicles, 2003.
7. Priestland, David. *The red flag: A history of communism*. Open Road+ Grove/Atlantic, 2016.

Index[1]

[1] Note: Page numbers followed by 'n' refer to notes.

R. Samuels, *Zizek and the Rhetorical Unconscious*,
https://doi.org/10.1007/978-3-030-50910-1